THE DEPARTMENT CHAIR PRIMER

What Chairs Need to Know and Do to Make a Difference

Second Edition

Don Chu

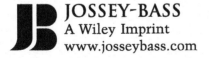

JOSSEY-BASS
A Wiley Imprint
www.josseybass.com

Published by Jossey-Bass
A Wiley Imprint
One Montgomery Street, Suite 1200, San Francisco, CA 94104-4594—www.josseybass.com

Jossey-Bass books and products are available through most bookstores. To contact Jossey-Bass directly
call our Customer Care Department within the U.S. at 800-956-7739, outside the U.S. at 317-572-3986,
or fax 317-572-4002.

Wiley publishes in a variety of print and electronic formats and by print-on-demand. Some material
included with standard print versions of this book may not be included in e-books or in print-on-
demand. If this book refers to media such as a CD or DVD that is not included in the version you
purchased, you may download this material at http://booksupport.wiley.com. For more information
about Wiley products, visit www.wiley.com.

Library of Congress Cataloging-in-Publication Data
Chu, Donald. date.
  The department chair primer : what chairs need to know and do to make a difference /
Don Chu.—2nd ed.
      p. cm.—(Jossey-Bass resources for department chairs)
  Includes references and index.
  ISBN 978-1-118-07744-3 (pbk.); 978-1-118-17343-5 (ebk); 978-1-118-17344-2 (ebk);
  978-1-118-17345-9 (ebk)
  1. College department heads. 2. Universities and colleges—Departments.   I. Title.
  LB2341.C543 2012
  378.1'11—dc23

                                                    23 2011038827

REVISED EDITION
PB Printing   10 9 8 7 6 5 4 3 2

CONTENTS

This book is dedicated
to those who hold most dear honor, loyalty, service, and integrity:
to my parents, who taught me these principles;
to my children, who carry forward these virtues;
and to my wife, Janine, whose love reminds me why they are
so important.

Preface to the New Edition

This is a book for academic leaders who are almost certainly too busy to read it—new department chairs. Chairs tell researchers that when they make the switch from faculty member to administrator, this transition into a brand new role takes up so much of their daily focus that they don't have the time or energy for much of anything else. Most say it takes them a year or even two before they feel that their feet are on the ground. Having been a department chair myself, I understand how important it is to get up to speed quickly and start doing the job. And not just for our own sake: chairs have never been more important to our departments, to our faculty, to our students, and to the community and society we serve in higher education than we are today.

The department chair is a change agent, the critical link in leadership that can lead to significant and almost immediate positive changes in higher educational institutions. In philosophy and sociology, the concept of "agency" is the capacity of individuals to make choices, to act on the world to change it. Gone are the days when chairs could wait out their terms, just do what had always been done, and assume that staff and historical protocol will keep the ship sailing on calm seas. To be successful in challenging times such as these, chairs need to be prepared for the job.

Our roles and responsibilities have shifted away from what they have been throughout our careers. As faculty, we may spend decades immersed in the culture and norms of behavior of our disciplines. We learn to analyze and write, to prepare and teach. We learn the language and customs of our disciplinary homes. But most new chairs take on this administrative job—in addition to their teaching duties—with little or no training. No wonder that new administrators so often feel at sea.

Chairs turn over rapidly in colleges and universities. Research shows that about half of all chairs turn over every three to six years (Chu and Veregge, 2002). For higher education to fulfill its vital social mission, department leaders must be prepared for their positions by getting up to speed on the basics quickly, educating themselves about the new role, and continuing to learn on the job. Chairs can actively manage and lead to improve the quality and productivity in higher education. The role of chair can be learned.

WHAT'S NEW IN THIS EDITION

This revision of *The Department Chair Primer* provides new administrators with what they need in an easily accessible form. These pages give you the context you need to get started and are full of practical ideas, examples, and possibilities for actions that you can take to make a difference. If you have the time and inclination to learn more about chairing, the Resources section at the back of the book lists some of the best of a growing list of references for theoretical and conceptual enrichment.

This book is divided into two parts. Part One provides the basics that you need to know as a front-line member of your institution's leadership and management team. Part Two is an overview of steps you can take to make good things happen in your department. Chapter Fourteen provides questions that you—as an individual or as part of a team of chairs—can work through to deepen your understanding of what you face and what actions you might take, given the particulars of your department and the environment in which it operates.

The landscape of higher education is changing rapidly and dramatically. Increasingly, more and more chairs are eager to create a culture of leadership and responsibility—to make a difference. I hope you will consider this new edition of *The Department Chair Primer* your guide in your new role as leader and your ongoing charge to make your department the best it can be for the faculty, staff, and students we all we serve.

California State University, San Marcos   DON CHU
October 2011

PART ONE

WHAT NEW CHAIRS
NEED TO KNOW

"We are so fortunate to have you in our department," the department chair said, welcoming the new faculty member. "We have high hopes for your work and the effect it may have on our students, your scholarly specialization, and the development of our service region. As your department chair, what I can do to support you and your work?"

How many of us had the good fortune to have an administrator who asked, "What do you need to help you in your work? What can I do for you to ease your transition?" Most of us—myself included—were pretty much left on our own to navigate this new territory.

As department chairs, we have the opportunity—and the responsibility—to be catalysts for the development of our faculty's talent; to be proactive supporters of good work to benefit our students and our scholarship; and to help those to whom we are obligated by our missions to serve. By applying the intelligence, analytical skills, discipline, and commitment to service that have made us successful in our careers as faculty, we can become excellent department chairs. But whereas it took us years or even decades to learn the art and science of scholarship and teaching, we do not have the luxury of time to learn the ins and outs of department administration.

The challenge facing new chairs today is to be able to make wise decisions from their very first day on the job. Not only do chairs have to make decisions about personnel, policies, and budget, but they also—perhaps literally overnight—must become the public and professional face of their unit. The chapters in Part One will provide you with the basic information you need to understand your role and negotiate your environment as you begin your new job.

CHAPTER ONE

WHY DEPARTMENT CHAIRS ARE IMPORTANT

The new chair of the Art History Department was looking forward to taking charge of her new responsibilities. She thought she could make a difference in her department, which had always seemed to her to be stuck in the past. She was surprised to hear her predecessor speak bitterly of his time in the office. "I never wanted this job," said Professor Ferguson, gathering his box of papers. "It was my turn," he shrugged. "Now it's yours. Good luck!"

Not so long ago, many department chairs like Professor Ferguson got the job because "it was their turn." Chairing the department was seen as a chore, a minor nuisance that got in their way until they had served their time. Some departments rewarded those who were willing to take on these management chores with tacit permission to support and forward their own specialization. Other chairs were expected simply to echo the dean's opinions or to blindly sign off on a course schedule that was the same every year, pass along "administrivia," and not get in the way. Inevitably, after a year or two, they finally learn enough about budgeting, resource management and development, personnel development, and curriculum and course scheduling to do their jobs effectively—but then it was time to give up the job to someone else . . . who also felt unknowledgeable and uncomfortable, unprepared to actively lead their units (Chu and Veregge, 2002).

Thankfully, times have changed. The contemporary mission of most department chairs is much more active and demanding. As higher education faces economic and social challenges, as administration is flattened due to budget cuts, and as competition for students and funding grows, chairs have increasingly found themselves in the center of the action.

Research tells us that very few chairs today agree to take on the job because they want power. It's not a career choice. It's a choice based on the need to serve their students, their colleagues, and the disciplines they represent. There is no one better positioned than the chair to do what is right and necessary for the department.

CASE STUDY: A SUCCESSFUL DEPARTMENT CHAIR

Department chairs have probably never been as important as they are today. In some ways, as you will learn, the position of department chair is more powerful than that of chancellor because it offers the very real opportunity to get things done. The following case study illustrates the significance of effective chair leadership

Dr. Li has been teaching in the Department of Mathematics for over twenty years. During that time, he has risen through the ranks, earning tenure and promotion to full professor along the way. Dr. Li has always been a tireless worker, teaching what needs to be offered, serving on countless committees without complaint, and advising multitudes of majors, all while gaining recognition for his applied mathematics scholarship.

Before he became chair several years ago, the department felt pressure from the all too common problems facing many academic departments today. As Chair Li put it, "Even before the recession, it didn't seem as if we could get enough faculty to teach all the courses everyone wanted us to teach. With so much to do, it was difficult for any of the faculty to do anything other than just teach. There was so little time to do research or to complete grant proposals. All of the faculty felt like rats on a treadmill, just running and running with no way to stop. The faster we ran, it seemed, the faster we needed to go just to keep from falling off."

In the twenty years that Professor Li has been in the department, he has heard many of his fellow faculty complain about the lack of support and respect for mathematics. "They would say, 'How can we do anything when we aren't supported?'" So when Dr. Li became chair, he decided to do something about it. He knew that the important problems facing his department could not be solved using the same level of thinking that was used to create those problems. It was time to engage both creatively and proactively.

First, he carefully analyzed his expenditures and made sure his budget was being used efficiently. He found that the department was being charged for many office and lab landline phones. Because these phones were barely used, he had them disconnected, saving about $2,000 per year. He then convinced the dean to allow him to redirect these funds into the purchase of laptop computers specially configured to assist the faculty with their instruction. Every year, he had a $2,000 fund to invest because this money was no longer being wasted on unused phone rental fees. "It wasn't rocket science," he explains. "I just had to do it. It wasn't difficult. It should have been done long ago."

The next step in his resource review was to look at the curriculum and course schedule. "We revised some of our lower-division courses to make them much more efficient," he says. "We produced the same enrollment with five or six fewer sections. This saved us lots of money that would have been used to pay adjuncts. I was able to convince the dean to allow us to use this money for travel to read for my faculty."

Dr. Li also engaged technology to help his faculty teach the basic college mathematics series. By adding hybrid and online courses to complement the face-to-face courses, he freed a number of his full-time faculty from the schedules they had been tied to for decades. "My faculty could put their lectures and PowerPoints online either synchronously or asynchronously, which was more attractive to their students. Because the faculty see each student's work, there is more interaction with individual students. Students could no longer hide in our traditional face-to-face sections by keeping their heads down so as to appear that they were working. Professors could actually see what each student was or was not doing."

Enrollments have increased markedly as students who work full time are able to fit classes into their work and family schedules. "We've seen more student satisfaction because students get more individual feedback in some part due to the laptops purchased for the faculty. These allow the faculty to correct formulas and equations easily and allow students to see the corrections almost immediately. Students no longer go off on the wrong track for entire class sessions and get further and further behind as much as they used to." Chair Li is able to schedule fewer sections because the popularity of courses offered through multiple technologies ensures that the sections that are offered are filled to capacity. He says, "I don't have faculty getting to their 8:00 A.M. and 5:00 P.M. classes only to find less than half the seats filled on Mondays and Fridays."

With some of the money he saved by pruning his course schedule, Chair Li has been able to hire graduate assistants to help his faculty with the lower-level math courses. He discovered that there have been students interested in graduate work in math for some time; by funding them with teaching assistantships, what had been an almost nonexistent graduate program has blossomed in numbers and excitement. "Most of the math problems lower-division students face are the same year in and year out. Training graduate students to work through these problems with them freed up my faculty to do much more advanced work, including their own research."

He adds, "We have a research culture developing between my faculty, who can now do more of their own research, and the students, who are excited to be learning how to teach math and who can help the faculty with advanced mathematics. It's becoming fun again."

Now that the faculty have more schedule flexibility and research assistance, they have begun reaching out more to other departments and to funding agencies that can help them with their research. "My faculty members don't feel that they are on the treadmill anymore. They have the time, and I have some funds to support them. They have always loved teaching, but now they feel that they are professors once more."

But perhaps the most important variable in this successful algorithm for department improvement has been Dr. Li's willingness to serve his faculty and students. "My faculty members see that I am teaching courses that I don't have to teach. They see me supporting their work more than just trying to build up my own specialization. They see me engaged in curriculum reform and putting in the hours it takes to improve student learning.

When they see me do this, they are willing to support me and the changes I am making to improve our department for the future."

What has been the result? Within three years of Dr. Li's leadership, his department—which had languished in the bottom of the rankings for years—has risen to the top of the state university system's rankings of student success in general studies mathematics preparation. Major numbers have risen significantly, and graduate enrollments have shot through the roof. Whereas math had been seen as a problematic department before Dr. Li assumed the chair's position, it is now seen as a model of efficiency and productivity. All of this has been accomplished with the same or less overall budget and numbers of faculty.

Reflecting on his first years in administration, Chair Li says, "I am surprised that more departments don't do what we have done. It is not a mysterious formula. It is mostly determining what works for the faculty and students and what has not worked. It has involved changing course schedules and faculty workload, and that took some getting used to; but the rewards have been immediate and obvious. Working in the same fiscal environment and under the same budgetary restrictions as other departments within the same college, we have accomplished much more than most of them. My colleagues throughout our college have noticed the changes. Other department chairs have asked me how we did this—how we changed both the effectiveness of our teaching and our productivity as scholars, but also how we have revitalized the spirit of the department. We wanted to do things better, and that's what we have achieved. We are all very proud."

A FORMULA FOR SUCCESS

In Dr. Li's department, the difference has been the chair. His formula for success was simple and elegant:

- He chose to lead and learned how to do it.
- He gained faculty support by leveraging the respect he had earned with them through his selfless service.
- He carefully analyzed the current budget, curriculum, and course schedule to maximize productivity (in the way of enrollments and quality student learning) and reduce costs.

- He gained the support of the dean to reinvest his department's money in technology, graduate students, and professional development that would build the strength of the department in the future.

Chair Li is a hardworking scientist who wants to do his part to advance his students, his department, and his university and to contribute his scholarship. In that way, he is like almost every college faculty member. As a chair, however, it is his willingness to lead that makes him stand out. He engaged the same qualities of intelligence, energy, and persistence that he used to earn his terminal degree and put them to work to help his department colleagues and students.

"The chair is responsible," he says, explaining why he took his leadership of the department so seriously. "If I had looked the other way or done nothing or just signed off and didn't try to make things better for my colleagues and students—if I didn't do something to try to make things better—then I was part of the problem."

Importantly, he assumed responsibility for managing efficiently and leading his department toward higher levels of achievement. He also put the time in to learn the mechanics of organizational management and leadership. Chair Li puts it in mathematic terms: "Before you can do calculus, you must learn to do basic algebra."

CHAPTER TWO

THE CHAIR'S ROLE AS DEPARTMENT LEADER

Professor Larsen was gratified to be given the department chair position, but he was a bit concerned too. "Great to hear you're going to going to be our new leader," said one of his longtime colleagues. "Now maybe we'll get something done around here for a change!" Professor Larsen wasn't so sure. He and his fellow faculty had complained for years about a curriculum in serious need of updating, and large numbers of good ideas have died an untimely death at the door of the previous chair's office. Larsen was full of energy and good intentions, but he wondered, "Can I really do anything new here? What power do I really have in this institutional machine?"

The rate of change in educational institutions often seems glacial. Stephen Portch, former chancellor of the University of Georgia, laments, "You can change the course of history more easily than you can change a history course." Institutions today are siloed into divisions: academic, business, student, and advancement affairs. Within severely constrained budgets and political alliances, real change is often problematic. The fallback position at the institutional level is to hunker down and defend what is already there. Seemingly powerful, chancellors occupy a highly visible political position, answerable to innumerable outside forces.

State funding for public institutions is down, and competition for federal, foundation, and private resources is increasing. As tuition and fees are ratcheted up to make up the shortfall, students and their financial supporters are quickly reaching the limits of their capacity to pay. Student debt is piling up, casting a pall over the formerly bright future of college graduates. Student demographics are changing; retraining and retooling are becoming more important for the changing workforce that cannot attend class Mondays through Fridays from 8:00 A.M. to 5:00 P.M.

Outcomes assessment and accountability are replacing the "logic of good faith" (Meyer and Rowan, 1977). Faculty and departments are being held increasingly accountable for their graduation rates and return on investment. Each and every faculty member in Texas, for example, is being rated on how much they bring in by the number of students they teach and their external funding versus how much they cost in the way of salary and expenses. States are demanding that institutions of higher education show that the taxpayers' money is being well spent.

For all these reasons, departments and their chairs are becoming more and more essential to the colleges and universities that serve their students and society. Responsiveness requires agility, and it is chairs who have their hands on the steering wheel of department operations. Department chairs, with the support of their faculty and dean, have much more latitude to formulate a vision, make decisions, and carry them through. Department chairs can actually have more influence over their departments and respond to pressing issues than chancellors do.

As the environment of higher education becomes more complex and diverse, department-level action provides the means to navigate nimbly and address the challenges facing our students, constituents, and institutions. As the official manager of the academic unit, the chair is ideally placed to mobilize the department to work with partners within and outside of the institution.

THE CATALYST BETWEEN IDEAS AND ACTION

As department chair, you are the first line of organizational management and leadership in higher education. You may not be able to change history, but you can change the courses taught in your department. If you, your faculty, or students have a workable new idea, you are perfectly positioned to put it into action.

Department chairs who can recognize worthy concepts can further the growth of these new ideas into useful course sections, classes, curriculum, projects, or programs. It's not up to you to come up with every new idea, but it is your responsibility to encourage faculty to bring new ideas forward. Because you are the chair, you can recognize ideas that have a future and bring them to light and the campus and public eye even when faculty may not know how to do so.

The chair's support of students and faculty can have an immediate impact on department spirit, faculty satisfaction, and the student experience. Because it is typically the faculty whose intellect and passion create new ways to address important problems, initiatives typically arise from the department level. Chairs need to encourage their faculty to think creatively—especially about things that you know have been bothering them for years and that they may be able to improve.

SETTING THE DEPARTMENT AGENDA

Chairs are authorized to set the department agenda. They can prioritize department goals, connect ideas with the individuals capable of putting them into action, and marshal resources to seed and nurture needed program and personnel changes.

For example, one of Chair Rosen's Education Department faculty came to him with a new approach to reach working adults who were unable to take time off from their jobs to complete their high school equivalency diplomas. She proposed creating a weekend adult school in the local community and staffing the program with education master's students from the university who were also certified teachers. Chair Rosen saw immediately how this plan could benefit the school, the students, and the community and gave her the go-ahead to come up with a detailed proposal.

In thinking about the plan, Chair Rosen also realized that working with adult learners would be an important service to the community and an area of applied scholarship that would be recognized in tenure and promotion reviews. He saw that it would make it possible to bring together university faculty who share an interest in working with adult high school noncompleters, to arrange productive meetings with school district and school board members, to free up some faculty time to work on this project by providing one course release, and to allocate graduate student assistance appropriately.

Eventually, the department, faculty, students, and community all became actively involved in the project, and most wondered why they hadn't done it sooner. Chair Rosen and his department eventually received official institutional and city recognition. Yet if the chair had not seen the wisdom in his faculty member's plan and understood his own power as leader, he would not have taken any action, and the concept would have fizzled.

Astute chairs will discover many opportunities to connect ideas, faculty, and resources to develop new programs, further initiatives, and address the needs of students, the department, the institution, and its constituencies. As Chair Rosen did, department heads can legitimize ideas, place projects high on the department agenda, and mobilize support to actualize what might otherwise remain conceptual.

For example, a psychology department chair might take a faculty member's research interest in, say, autism and create program teams to work with community mental health providers both to deliver client services and to develop grant proposals to further good works and research in this area of study. Thanks to the chair's position within the institution, meetings with significant mental health professionals can be arranged, dialogue with interested faculty in other departments can be facilitated, students can obtain both curriculum and clinical experience, and research and service to autistic populations and their support groups can be developed. Without the chair's support, the faculty member's research interest would probably remain just that and never evolve into a program area of enormous benefit.

FACULTY AS A DEPARTMENT RESOURCE

Talented faculty are the engine of higher education, and workload changes affect the department's work and impact. What faculty focus on in their work is the major resource available to the department and institution.

Chairs have the power to shift faculty workload and in so doing to change department priorities. For example, by shifting a faculty member's workload from what is normally a four-course teaching load to a three-course teaching load supplemented by a one-course directed assignment to develop curriculum for a new program, chairs may shift 25 percent of the faculty workload in order to meet new student needs.

Curriculum and Coursework

Curriculum and coursework are the heart of higher education, and curriculum is made by the department faculty. The tradition of academic freedom maintains that curriculum, the courses that constitute majors and minors, and options must be approved at the department level. The chair usually speaks for the department.

The chair can support or table curriculum proposals or relegate them to the fate of "death by committee." A faculty idea to develop a new minor in Japanese studies, for instance, can go nowhere if the chair is unwilling to approve it or is "too busy" to transmit it to the next committee or next-level officer.

Chairs can also draft new curricula and coursework or authorize other faculty to do so. Chairs may decide to bring new curricula to the table for discussion and review and, after approvals, implement new courses, majors, minors, certificates, and program emphases.

The courses your department offers have a real impact on students. How often courses are offered, the instructional mode in which they are offered, and course content directly affect individual students. So does the person you choose to teach your most significant courses. Chairs must carefully choose the teachers of the most important courses, weighing who has taught them in the past as well as who would teach them best.

For example, the new Religious Studies Chair, Professor Ramirez, was reviewing a longstanding general education course in comparative religion that focused on Western religions. She knew it had the power to make a certain impact on general studies students and began thinking about it in the context of what she knew about the student body and the direction of religious studies today. She decided to suggest to the faculty teaching that course that it might need updating to better align with student interest in non-Western traditions and current social conditions. Despite initial resistance from the faculty member who had been teaching the course for more than a decade, Chair Ramirez followed up closely, knowing that her suggestion and this change could have a significant impact on students for decades to come.

TENURE AND PROMOTION

Faculty tenure and promotion decisions chart the course of the future for generations—and these decisions start with the department. The chair's evaluation is a crucial piece in the determination of the composition of the faculty who will shape the future of students, your department, and the institution.

Chairs are responsible for knowing the future of the discipline represented in their department and how well individual faculty fit into making the curriculum, service, and scholarship right for the future. A chair who recommends a particular faculty member for tenure, for example, is in essence saying that this person will make necessary contributions in the way of scholarship, teaching, and service for the next several decades and that this potential investment of possibly several million dollars over the lifetime of the faculty member is worth making.

HIRING

Hiring decisions may seem seem like a simple, short-term issue, but hiring is an investment of well over $1 million over the course of a faculty member's career. Decisions chairs make in the hiring process usually extend far beyond their tenure as department leaders. Good hiring decisions position a department for a bright future.

Hiring starts with the department. Faculty lines are precious, especially in the current economic climate. When a vacancy arises or if a new line becomes available, it is critical that the highest department priorities be reflected in the vacancy description and in position announcements.

As chair, you have the authority to develop the vacancy description and the search committee. Consider these issues with care: Should a replacement be hired in precisely the area from which the retirement occurs? What will be the greatest department need for the next twenty to thirty years? Who will be on the search committee? Who will get to communicate with potential hires about what the department is all about and where it is headed?

PURSUING A LEADERSHIP ROLE

Most of us chose careers in higher education because we wanted to contribute. Our research helped expand the scholarly foundations of our subject matter. Our teaching passed knowledge on to future generations. Service to our professions, as well as to our constituents, permitted us to make a direct impact on those we served. As department chair, this is your chance to make all this happen. Through proactive leadership, chairs may develop faculty talent and connect talent with the needs of the constituencies we serve. Chairs break down boundaries, getting our talented faculty and staff out of silos and into the wider community on and off campus. Chairs who choose to lead can be key players in advancing the interests of the faculty, our students, and our communities.

CHAPTER THREE

THE CHAIR'S ECOSYSTEM

After greeting his office staff on the first day as department chair, Chair Matsuura entered his office to find a rather alien environment. Instead of journals, research software, class lists, and grade sheets, the new chair found piles of memos, institutional studies, committee report requests—and deadlines. As he was looking around, trying to make sense of his cluttered desk to find the computer, his administrative assistant appeared to announce three meetings on the day's agenda for which he was completely unprepared. And then the phone started ringing.

It is not uncommon for new chairs to walk in on the first day of work with no formal preparation for their new role. Like Chair Matsuura, you may feel that you have entered a bewildering new world. Rather than academic terms organized around Monday-Wednesday and Tuesday-Thursday classes, the chair's year is chopped up by a seemingly endless stream of meetings of every sort. In your years as a professor, you have learned to see your department from the narrow perspective of a faculty member. Suddenly, your position is very different—and the way you experience the department and its context in the institution will also be different.

As noted earlier, research shows that it may take a year or two before new chairs feel that their feet are on the ground (Chu and Veregge, 2002)—but you don't have that long. Understanding the ecosystem in which chairs operate will speed up your familiarization process, allowing you to move quickly and with more assurance. Before beginning the new role, it's vital to understand the system and the chair's place in it.

OPERATING IN AN OPEN SYSTEM

For the most part, faculty focus on their own work—teaching their classes, taking care of their students, conducting their research, writing their articles, drafting their grant proposals, and serving their regional and professional organizations. As faculty, you have come to regard your department as a closed system: the factors important to your work are wholly contained in that department—the students and the physical and financial resources needed for teaching, scholarship, and service. Like a self-contained family, members of that small organization assume it to be the most important environment that affects their work. Figure 3.1 shows what a closed system looks like.

But as chair, your department is an open system. This perspective assumes that the factors important to the work of the department are contained both within the unit and also in the unit's "task environment," which possesses the resources needed by the department and also wants what the department can provide. Figure 3.2 shows how this open system might be conceptualized.

Operating in a Task Environment

The task environment is so called because without the support of the constituents in the unit's environment, the department cannot effectively perform the essential tasks that are its reason for being. For example, one important element in the task environment is

FIGURE 3.1. THE DEPARTMENT AS A CLOSED SYSTEM.

ACADEMIC DEPARTMENT
|
Primary constituent: students
|
Productive engine: faculty and staff
|
Resources needed for production: budget allocation, facilities, and equipment
|
Products: curriculum, faculty scholarship

FIGURE 3.2.   THE DEPARTMENT AS AN OPEN SYSTEM.

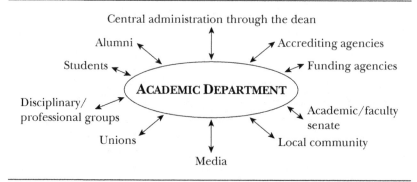

the department's accrediting agency. In the quid pro quo relationship between the department and this critical member of its task environment, the department provides qualified faculty, curriculum and coursework, student supports, and institutional support as expected by the accrediting body. In return, the department gets accreditation as a seal of approval.

Another example of this exchange relationship is the federal, state, and other bodies that need research, assessment, policy papers, and contract work performed. Faculty typically do this work with their colleagues and students. In return, the funding agency provides resources for the department and funding for student labor, the principal investigators, and directors, as well as indirect return to the institution.

Operating in a Bureaucracy

Most colleges and universities are organized as bureaucracies. Although they may benefit from a tradition of shared governance, a culture that values transparency and open communication, and legal responsibility to government entities and governing boards, colleges and universities are still bureaucracies.

As such, they are organized around a structure of subunits in the organization, each of which is specialized to perform its own particular function. Each subunit is headed by a chair, director, or other officer who is primarily responsible for its operations. Information and authority flow through that head of the subunit, who is responsible to sign off on decisions made for that entity.

What this all means at the department level is that the chair is the chief officer responsible to manage his or her subunit. Furthermore, chairs are the chief boundary spanners. Chairs may stand between or bring together the department's faculty, students, and staff and both the internal and external constituencies.

The Chair as Chief Boundary Spanner

It is, of course, possible to be a department chair without ever venturing beyond the narrow confines of the office. But chairs who understand their role as leaders and boundary spanners will reach out to other departments in the institution, as well as to community, state, and federal organizations, to discover their needs. Often these chairs discover that other constituencies are thankful for the effort and willing to fund responses that can only come from the department's talented faculty and students.

The boundary spanner role is vital with internal constituencies. For example, the Engineering Department chair can say to the Mathematics Department chair, "No, we will not accept that course that you are planning to offer because it is too close to our curriculum and what we are charged to do." Or that chair can say, "We are grateful that you are planning to offer that course, and as a matter of fact, we would like to require that course for our majors as an option every other year. By doing so, we will be able to offer another course for our majors because we will not have to offer our previous requirement."

In speaking on behalf of the department to external constituents, the chair can explore new connections. For example, the chair might say to a community organization proposing a partnership, "That's a very interesting idea. Why don't we form a group to look at how we can help you? We'll see if we can marshal the resources inside our department and institution to make that happen." By connecting the department faculty with organizations or groups in need, the chair is not only lining up possible funding but also fulfilling the institution's service mission.

As the official boundary spanners for their departments, chairs can position their faculty with community organizations and funding agencies. Chairs can be on the lookout for grants and contracts that match the talents and needs of their faculty. By working directly with their research office, they can communicate with funding sources and match faculty with program officers in federal, state, and local agencies.

The structural walls imposed by bureaucracy are making the chair's function as boundary spanner increasingly important. Technology has globalized and flattened the world of higher education, bringing both opportunities and threats to the department's doorstep. Individual chairs, of course, may see this work as outside of what they signed on to do. If you feel resistant, give it time and think about the possibilities. The chair's ability and willingness to reach across boundaries to grasp opportunities and to defend against challenges will be a hallmark of contemporary chair success.

WHAT CHAIRS NEED TO KNOW ABOUT FACULTY

The most important thing you need to know about faculty is this: for the duration of your time as department chair, you can no longer see things only from their perspective. As you assume the chair, you instantly become a member of a much larger world. Chairs work between and on behalf of the department's faculty, staff, and students, on the one hand, and everyone else outside of the institution who wants something from the department, on the other. Necessarily, your understanding of faculty and your relationship to them must change.

Being "One of the People"

Although some chairs are brought in from the outside, most chairs come from the department's faculty. Thus chairs are "one of the people"—they are familiar with the other faculty and staff, have probably developed their careers side by side, and to a degree are personally familiar with the faculty and their stories.

Owing to their personal and professional proximity to their colleagues and also to the likelihood that they will return to the faculty in the same department, chairs promoted from within are in position to encourage more lasting changes than those imposed from above or outside. There is a Chinese expression that says, "The people will always win." Despite the imposed will of emperors and autocrats, the saying goes, the people will win in the end because they will merely pay lip service and wait out changes that they do not agree with and that they do not feel are in their best interests.

What's more, the department chair has a power of persuasion that can come from knowing the personal agendas and professional aspirations of their once and future faculty.

A Quid Pro Quo Relationship

Faculty and chair are in a quid pro quo relationship: faculty provide their expertise in return for what the task environment can provide to them or their department. The most basic of these is the teacher-student relationship: faculty members teach, and students provide their enrollment. Faculty serve the institution well, and in return, they receive a salary and career support.

For many department chairs, the greatest joy in their position is helping the faculty improve their teaching, scholarship, or service. The chairs' unique position as boundary spanners for their departments allows them to connect faculty with colleagues, with professionals in the community and across the country, and with community and regional constituents who can benefit from the faculty's expertise. In the best of administrative worlds, chairs facilitate the good work of the faculty and help them grow, which excites them and elevates their professional stature. This in turn energizes the chair, who sees that administration can be productive, meaningful, and even exciting. When administrators sense that they have had something to do in the expansion of the good works of the department, it nourishes a sense of purpose and strengthens motivation for the future.

Understanding the "Normal Distribution" of Faculty Members

We would like to believe that all of our faculty will hold their students, scholarship, and service to others above all else and that they will tailor their behavior so as to maximize those benefits to others. Yet most chairs are experienced enough to know that this will not always be the case.

The range of department faculty pretty much follows the "normal distribution." Most faculty will be somewhere around the mean insofar as their performance is concerned; a smaller number will be stars in their field and positive influences in the department. And almost without fail, a small group of others may fall on the negative end of the distribution. Often these are the ones who make the most noise and capture an inordinate amount of attention.

David Perlmutter, in an article titled "Spotting Your Enemies," describes a number of faculty types to beware of. "Turfmasters" are fine so long as chairs don't tread on their sacred territory—that is, their assignments, allocations, positions, and status. "Prickly pears" have huge chips on their shoulders, and their insecurity drives them to battle every perceived slight to their prestige. "Big bullies" make almost everyone's life miserable. Their best friends are their lawyers, whom they allege get rich from every threatened lawsuit. "Dr. Chaos" enjoys conflict and stirs up trouble, blaming everyone else for how horrible the world is. "Deal makers" look out for themselves and try to cut deals to their benefit even if unfair to others. "Smilers" grin to your face. They may be pleasant and gracious publicly, but they are sneaky and deceitful. Their main weapon is often character assassination.

Fortunately, the majority of faculty will make significant contributions to the department and the institution, but it is not always the majority who are most salient. In any office cluster, there will be rivalries and jealousies. Be aware that some negativity will likely come your way, and understand that the naysayers are probably not speaking for the majority.

WHAT CHAIRS NEED TO KNOW ABOUT DEANS

Deans are very different from chairs in one crucial way: their career aspirations. Seeking a deanship is often a well-thought-out decision. It is a move that says, "I seek a career in higher education administration," and many deans choose to travel the administrative route in the hope of climbing far up the administrative ladder. In contrast, most chairs are simply fulfilling their responsibility to the department and expect to return to the faculty. In many significant ways, however, the environment in which deans operate resembles the chair's world.

Where Deans Operate

Deans operate in the middle—between the chair and the administrative vice president. All institutional deans have fiduciary responsibility to manage their own departments, to efficiently employ institutional resources and budget to achieve institutional objectives.

In some institutions, budgeting and resources are relatively stable, with adjustments made on a pro rata basis depending on the percentage of the institutional budget each college receives. That is, if College X has historically received an allocation of 20 percent of the institutional budget, should the institution suffer a $10 million reduction, it would lose $2 million of its allocation. Other college deans may work in a zero-based budgeting system in which they have to compete for funding by providing evidence for the value and productivity of their college's departments. Clearly this would be a much more competitive budget environment.

When we apply the open-systems perspective to the dean's world, we see that the most important person in the task environment is the academic vice president (AVP) to whom the dean reports. In most cases, it is the AVP's evaluation that matters the most. If the AVP believes that the dean is effective, that's good for the dean. If the AVP sees the dean as weak, ineffective, or not working well as a member of the "senior administrative leadership team," the dean's effectiveness may be limited. That dean may have a short career, in the AVP's estimation.

How Deans Are Like Chairs

Like chairs, deans generally receive little training before they become deans. Most have been chairs or assistant or associate deans, but these jobs do not prepare new deans for the pressures, anxieties, and opportunities associated with being in such a public position and responsible for such a large burden of management and control. Most deans, like chairs, learn on the job. Most deans, like chairs, do want to help, but they may not know early in their careers how to help. Like chairs, deans do make mistakes, and most learn from their mistakes.

The problem for deans is that they are in a more public position, and second chances are harder to come by. Deans (like everyone higher in central administration) are generally hired and employed, in contractual terms, "at the pleasure of the president." This means that they can be fired "without cause." Employed one day, gone the next. This is the reality of the dean's job, and it tends to make people in that position very cautious.

For both chairs and deans, it is an article of faith that for the most part anyone who chooses a career in higher education does so for the purpose of making a contribution. Both deans and chairs have some good colleagues who are easy to work with and who want to help them succeed; they also have colleagues who care less for others than themselves, their unit, and their careers. The same is true for vice presidents. Some truly work as team members and are willing to submerge their self-interests for the welfare of the institution and achievement of its mission. But then there are vice presidents who either know too little to help, know enough but don't want to help, or know enough and try to elevate themselves and their units for their own benefit.

There are many fewer deans than there are chairs, so deans are much more visible—and more vulnerable—than chairs. This factor will certainly color the decisions each of you will make. As one chair said philosophically, "What can they do to me if they don't like the job I'm doing? They can fire me and I become a faculty member—again, thank goodness!"

Why Deans Think Chairs Have a More Difficult Job

Most deans, vice presidents, and presidents find their jobs difficult in many ways—and for good reason. Yet many of them remark that in retrospect, the position of chair is the most difficult because so much of it is "personal."

As chair, you are working with your colleagues, many of whom you think of as friends. You have always been "on the same side." Although many faculty understand the role conflict and role stress under which the chair works, there will be some faculty who still take the chair's decisions personally. Yet as chair, you are faced with doing what is best for the department's students and the institution, even if the faculty grumble and even though chances are that after the chair's term ends, you will be faculty again—and maybe with an office next door to the new chair's.

Working Effectively with Faculty and Dean

Chairs and deans work in an ecosystem quite different from the libraries, labs, and classrooms that make up most of the faculty world. In this world, the extent to which chairs may lead is a direct result of their dean's willingness to endorse that leadership role.

As the bureaucracy's supervising officers, deans are obligated for the management of department affairs. Therefore, chairs who seek to lead their departments actively need to bear this in mind: all department administrative decisions pass through the dean. Chairs can lead and manage proactively only if they are permitted to do so by their dean.

When working with faculty and the dean, chairs need to keep the following points in mind:

• Chairs are the boundary spanners who connect the department and the faculty with the campus and community. Chairs need to look both within their departments as well as outside into the service region and national and international constituents so that they may connect faculty talents with those who need faculty expertise and skills on and off campus.

• Since most chairs have come from their faculty, the chairs' greatest strength is their knowledge of faculty (interests, motivation, expertise, skills), the department curriculum and course schedule, and the needs of students.

• In the department chair's "best world," the chair furthers the good work and professional growth of faculty, which in turn encourages the chair to continue doing so in the future. In the not-so-perfect real world, however, chairs must be on the lookout for the few faculty or staff who cast a negative shadow on other department members.

• Both deans and chairs are "middle managers." There is great diversity among deans insofar as their training, motivation, and effectiveness as managers and leaders goes. If chairs intend to lead and manage proactively, however, it is crucial that they be supported by their dean.

Chapter Four

Handling Stress and Conflict

Professor Iuzzo's husband was worried. When his wife assumed the position of chair of the Anthropology Department, she explained that she would probably need time to get up to speed on her new responsibilities. But what he saw was troubling: she always seemed to be at a meeting. She was grabbing meals on the run, spending late nights at the computer preparing for the next day, and sleeping poorly. She seemed distracted, and his normally even-tempered wife was uncharacteristically impatient with their children. When he tried to broach the subject, she waved him away, saying she just had no time to talk about it. He hoped that she'd be able to ease up soon, but he had already started counting the days until she could go back to teaching.

When new chairs are asked what most surprised them about the job, they cite "the amount of time the job takes" and "the amount of paperwork." Faculty are typically unaware of how much chairs have to do in order to represent their departments and work with their colleagues. The process takes time. Documentation carefully done takes hours and energy. Listening—on top of teaching and lecturing—takes time.

Next most surprising to new chairs is the number of meetings that they have to go to and the strain that chairing can put on their relationships with colleagues. It's important for your department to be at the table, so chairs need to take their seats and contribute. But shared governance and collaborative teams require meetings and more meetings (Chu and Veregge, 2002), and new relationships take time to develop and nurture. In the meantime, established relationships may suffer.

Significantly, while chairs are busy representing their departments in their new roles, they are not in their old roles as faculty peers. Evaluations and the authority to allocate and set workloads may place a strain on relationships developed over the years. Fiduciary responsibilities may strain old friendships and heighten faculty sensitivities. All of this can lead to stress and conflict.

HANDLING THE BUREAUCRATIC GRIND AND HOUSEKEEPING TASKS

Two responsibilities that typically take up a great deal of the chair's time are the "bureaucratic grind" and "housekeeping routine." The "bureaucratic grind" includes organizational tasks with which new administrators are typically not familiar: according to chairs, "reading and responding to memos from other offices," "writing reports," and "reading administratively relevant material" consume much of the day not already taken up by meetings.

The second set of tasks that take up so much of their time may be called the "household routine." Chairs must make sure that the academic house runs smoothly and that every chore is taken care of. Chores in this category of tasks include staffing classes, scheduling classes and rooms, recruiting staff and faculty, budget management and planning, and managing staff and faculty.

It takes time to become accustomed to the feel of the chair's role and the tasks that have to be performed. Chairs assuming the role at the beginning of the academic year in late August, for example, will learn that the budget for the upcoming academic year has probably already been established. They will learn that course schedules for fall are already set and that only minor tweaking is permitted because registration has largely taken place already. Come September or so, they will be asked to submit the spring term classes and learn that the classes for the upcoming term are pretty much the same classes that were taught the year before. Workload and end-of-year fiscal accounting begins about midway through the spring term, and book closing begins sometime around April.

All of this will be new the first year of the new chair's tenure, and the pattern will likely be repeated in the second year. Chairs generally feel more familiar with the schedule the second time around.

ROLE STRESS AND ROLE CONFLICT

With all the time the job takes and all the functions chairs need to be good at, it is not uncommon for chairs to feel two types of role pressure: "role stress" and "role conflict." Although both are common in the first year on the job, familiarity with the chair's responsibilities often reduces them thereafter.

Role Stress

Role stress is a result of too few hours in the day to do what needs to be done. In the course of workshops for new chairs, it is common to hear comments such as these:

"How in the world can anyone get everything done that needs to be done by the chair? There never seems to be enough time in the day!"

"I get into the office before 8:00 A.M. and leave every day after 5:00 P.M. I've still got reports and memos to read. Every day I get more and more e-mails, and they're stacked up in the pile waiting to be read. I'm getting awfully tired."

For brand new chairs who haven't figured out which tasks are truly important and the most efficient way to do their jobs, there just seems to be too much to do. Meetings alone can take up most of the hours in the day. Most chairs continue to teach, and some have graduate theses and dissertations to work on with their students. If the chair has a personal life—marriage, intimate relationships, children—it often suffers.

Fortunately, after the initial shock of the first year, chairs typically feel more comfortable with their jobs in succeeding years. With experience, role stress is often reduced as chairs learn to plan their days around the most important tasks, to prioritize, to delegate, and to use every available hour of the workday more efficiently. One helpful approach is to make friends with the best chairs in the institution. Tips from experienced chairs on how they handle their jobs can reduce the stress level for new chairs who are just learning the ropes.

Role Conflict

Role conflict results from parts of the job that seem to be at odds. For instance, administrators may sense conflict between what they perceive as the contradictory demands of boosting faculty but also evaluating them.

Chairs who have come from the faculty and who expect that they will return to the faculty may feel conflicted doing what they believe is in the best long-term interests of the department while fearing that such actions may upset or alienate their colleagues. Switching faculty offices and altering long-established teaching schedules or assignments are two examples of actions that can generate role conflict.

When faculty who have been teaching their pet courses have their schedules disturbed, this can lead to difficult times for the department chair—even if the chair is certain that the low enrollments and major counts in the faculty member's curriculum need attention. To some extent, role conflict is inevitable.

To minimize role conflict, it is important for chairs to understand that they assume this administrative position as a service to their colleagues and students. With their wider view of the department and its ecosystem within the campus and community, chairs often have a different perspective than colleagues who are happily focused on their own work. Here, communication is key: the entire department needs to understand the reasons for the chair's decisions and agenda. Chairs who base their actions on what is best for the long-term interests of the department are on more solid footing than administrators who make ad hoc decisions appealing to short-term interests and the comfort of a few.

CHAPTER FIVE

WHAT KIND OF CHAIR WILL YOU BE?

The Sociology Department faculty was buzzing about the choice of Professor Rajput as the chair. Some welcomed him as a strong leader and a positive change from the outgoing chair, who had merely maintained the status quo established by the previous chair. Others were afraid he was going to be taking his leadership role a bit too seriously. Things were going well, and they feared that in his enthusiasm, he might make wholesale changes that would disrupt their routine. For his part, Professor Rajput was all too aware that all eyes were on him—and he, too, wondered what kind of chair he would turn out to be.

As soon as new chairs are chosen—regardless of the officially designated start date—they have already begun to assume the status and authority of the new position in the eyes of their peers and fellow administrators. People are naturally concerned with how the chair will run the department, and they are watching closely. Chairs have oversight and management responsibilities, they are closer to central administration, and they have access to information other faculty do not have. As chair, it is important to act professionally at all times.

Higher education's historical roots are ecclesiastical and are marked by service to others. Chairs who favor their own specialization or their own friends and interests set a negative tone for department operations. There is no place for self-interest in the chair's office. Seize the opportunity offered by your colleagues' close observation, and model the commitment to service that you hope your own faculty, staff, and students will exhibit.

CONSTANT OBSERVATION

As chair, it is not enough to say to yourself, "I'll just be myself." You are, of course, the same person you were before your appointment; but layered on top of that identity is a new public identity as "the chair." Because you now represent something much bigger than yourself as an individual, your behavior must also reflect this greater responsibility as an officer of the institution.

You were once, and likely still are, faculty; but you are now also an administrator with authority over the fate of others. Although you may not see yourself as superior to your colleagues, you are different because you are now the chair, and people are watching to see just how different you will be.

You cannot control what others think and say about you, so chairs need to be aware of people's perceptions. Remember that you are under constant observation, always being watched and evaluated. Mind what you do and say. Pay attention to how you speak and act. Your tone and actions matter. The role requirements, expectations, and responsibilities of chairs are different from those of faculty. Expect to be treated differently as a result.

THE LONG VIEW

You are now the public face of your department, the guardian of the subject matter that should benefit your students and service area, and the chief administrator responsible for the unit. So it's important to resist jumping into decision making on the basis of the biases, attitudes, and ideas you developed as faculty.

New chairs especially can benefit from taking some time to understand competing points of view. Chairs represent the department and are members of the school administration, so it is important to demonstrate a broad understanding of the many positions and issues facing the institution, the department, and all of its faculty, staff, and students. Consider these multiple points of view before deciding on some course of action. Take time to think about multiple reference points before responding to a comment or question. Keep emotional responses to a minimum, and avoid belittling opinions that conflict with yours.

WHAT KIND OF CHAIR CAN YOU BE?

You can be whatever kind of chair you choose to be. During the course of my work with department leaders, I have had the pleasure of meeting a wide variety of chairs.

Small and Large Departments

Chairs of small departments (with no more than five full-time faculty) and chairs who work in small colleges (with perhaps a total of thirty to forty full-time faculty) may operate under protocols whereby the dean's office manages almost all operations of departments including scheduling, workload, and curriculum. In colleges such as these, chairs may make their greatest contributions by mentoring individual faculty and supporting their professional growth.

In larger colleges and in departments with around thirty or more full-time faculty, chairs may have much more authority to manage and lead their units. In such circumstances, the boundary-spanning responsibilities of chairs may be much greater. These chairs may need to connect with the community, engage national and professional leadership in the nonprofit and for-profit sectors, and fundraise and make friends for the department with its constituents.

Time to Adjust

Understanding the kind of chair you want to be may take some time. It will certainly take time for you to become comfortable with your new role. A professor's work is for the most part solitary—teaching and writing manuscripts. The work is stable, with a predictable workflow. Professors work within allocated budgets, and they work relatively independently, focusing on whatever was their top priority.

Chairing, in contrast, is a social position requiring a great deal of interaction both inside and outside of the department. Memos replace manuscripts. Chairs are the allocators rather than the recipients of allocations. Their time and focus are fragmented. Chairing is a service position in which fiduciary responsibility and selflessness replace the self-interest of focusing one's own career and research line. Chairs are the custodians of the department's contributions to others and to future generations (Gmelch, 2000).

Until that first learning year is over, chairs are overly busy with the whirlwind of meetings, a calendar that demands reports and evaluations by preset dates, curriculum that must be revised with new times, budgets that are ever shrinking or pulled in every direction for new dollars. They are kept so busy, in fact, that they often feel they have no time to devote to their own scholarship or their personal lives. It's difficult to learn the job, to place it in the broader institutional context, and to learn new approaches and options for department direction when every day is as full as your e-mail queue.

After the first year or so, new administrators begin to feel more comfortable with the basic requirements of this new role and are better able to refine their approach to department management and leadership. They have a more realistic idea as to which tasks are central and which are less important. They are able to poke their heads above water and see who the best chairs are on their campus, begin to model the actions of these leaders, and better determine for themselves the type of chair they want to be.

Like all administrators, chairs vary, falling anywhere on a spectrum for a number of dimensions such as these:

Change Agent————Caretaker

Dynamically Oriented————Stability Oriented

Internally Directed————Externally Directed

Institutional Leader————Faculty Servant

Clearly, successful chairs cannot tackle every issue facing their departments with equal vigor, and they cannot assume a position on one of the dimensions and stick to it in every circumstance. Limited resources will require prioritizing challenges. Changing times will also change the chair's approach. At one point, for example, a more sedate, stable approach is warranted, especially after periods of turbulence in the department. At other times, action will be necessary to help the department change to meet new challenges.

The Pleasure of the Dean

As new administrators zero in on the type of chair they want to be, it is also important to remember that chairs work under the authority of the dean of their college or director of their school. Chairs can only be as assertive and dynamic as the dean or director allows them to be. In some cases, the dynamism will come directly from the dean's office. At other times, a dean may be focused on other college issues and either want a chair to go slowly or defer some action that may be controversial.

A reality of bureaucratic organizations is that there is only so much that top-level administrators can focus on. There are only so many issues to which to apply their political capital and energy. Your dean may be focused on your department now or may turn to it later. It is always in the best interests of the chair and the department for chairs to gain the confidence of the dean and to clearly communicate department news, challenges, and plans.

PART TWO

GETTING STARTED: HOW NEW CHAIRS CAN MAKE A DIFFERENCE

It is common for new chairs to assume that "someone else will do it." But the truth of the matter is that, as in most of life, it is up to you.

There will never be enough administrative staff to do this work for you. There will never be enough resources to get what you believe is your fair share without working hard for them. There will never be enough marketing, admissions, and public relations staff to do all the work your department needs to get done. Even if there were enough staff, your colleagues in other departments will expect them to focus on their units and not yours.

Your dean has multiple departments to deal with. Your academic vice president has many colleges and their deans to deal with. Your president or chancellor has a great many community constituents, trustees, legislators, and donors to deal with.

This means that the department's future is primarily in the hands of the chair, the person who has immediate authority over the curriculum, course schedule, faculty workload, resource, and budget. You might as well get started, and get started right. Although the particulars of your department will determine the benefits of each action, even small steps can add up to make the department better now and in the future.

Part Two is a guide to the steps chairs can take to make a difference in the following important areas: planning; budget, resource management, and development; curriculum, scheduling, and instruction; professional development, personnel management, and challenging personnel; department communications; student development; and strategic positioning. The final chapter will give you a chance to reflect on your own institution and department and begin to plan for your future as chair. But first, we'll look at what you need to know before you begin to take action.

CHAPTER SIX

BEFORE YOU BEGIN

Over the decade she'd been teaching at the university, Dr. Young had thought in passing about how the History Department should be run or what she'd do if she were given the reins, but she'd never given much attention to these musings. Now, suddenly, it's her turn. She's been named chair, it's the beginning of August, and the academic year starts next week. She has little idea what to expect or what the job requires, and no one has given her any training. Over the years, she's thought to herself that the department's scholarship should be ramped up, but she doesn't have a very good idea how to do that. She did attempt to pick the brain of the outgoing chair, but he wasn't much help except to warn her to "watch your back." Now, as her new life as chair of the department was almost upon her, she wondered, "What do I do first?"

Like Dr. Young and so many other new chairs, you've spent years learning to be a professor—that's what you've trained for, it's what you know, and teaching is still part of your daily job responsibilities. But now you must also be an administrator—and all you see are question marks.

Fortunately, there is much you can do during this time to help you plant your feet more firmly on the ground. Take the time you need to prepare for your new role, think about your goals, and set a positive agenda and tone for the term and the terms to follow. The first step is to have a grasp of the fundamentals of your new role.

UNDERSTANDING THE EXPECTATIONS

As noted earlier, as chair you represent more than yourself: you represent your academic field, your profession, your faculty and staff, and your students. Your actions matter to others—now and in the future. That means working for the best interests of all the constituencies you represent. No longer are your own specialization, your own point of view, or your own present concerns and future your primary focus. You must look out for the best interests of your department in its entirety, and you are just about the only one who can do it. And the way to do it is to build bridges of communication with other offices both inside and outside of the educational institution.

Be on Good Terms with the Dean

How much good a chair can do to improve conditions for the department's students, faculty, and staff depends on how much authority the dean allows the chair to exercise. Some deans feel the need to approve just about everything, as if they were direct managers of the unit. Other deans authorize chairs to both manage and lead without much direct supervision. Regardless of where your institution falls in this structure, it's important to recognize and nurture this important relationship.

Understand the Chair's Fiduciary Responsibility

Chairs have a fiduciary responsibility to manage department assets, safeguard the rights of beneficiaries, and act in the best interests of the department. They are obligated to act on behalf of the students, faculty, and staff of the department and to protect and manage department assets on their behalf. Personal self-interests are secondary to this moral and legal obligation.

Maintain Confidentiality

Professorial culture is predicated on the sharing of ideas, but managers have additional responsibilities. As unit managers, chairs have access to a great deal of information about individuals and the organization. The privacy of individuals and the confidentiality of information need to be protected and assured.

Build and Maintain Credibility

Credibility may be the chair's greatest visible asset. Building and maintaining credibility is simple: do what you say you're going to do, and don't do what you say you won't do. Encourage trust by being trustworthy.

Manage "Opportunities," Not "Problems"

One person's "problem" is another person's "opportunity." Some faculty may see small classes as wonderful, but the chair may see low-enrollment sections as a burden in that the department is neither using its personnel dollars efficiently nor reaching all of the students it is responsible to serve.

Chairs need to be careful what they label a "problem" worthy of their time and attention. The capacity to triage the numerous issues they face every day and to determine which are "problems" worth confronting and which are really opportunities in disguise says a lot about the chairs' abilities.

Begin Thinking About Direction

Even if you don't know your exact destination when you first assume the chair position, you should at least begin to develop an idea of the direction in which you want to head. Dr. Young, for example, felt that scholarship was the direction she wanted to take in the History Department. She was not sure yet whether that would mean juried articles, funded research, or enlarged graduate enrollments, but just understanding that this was a priority for her gave her a core around which to begin planning what she might do during her tenure as chair.

Success also depends on being able to measure progress. For example, if the direction you head is toward growth of the department, is that measured by head count or full-time-equivalent students? If the direction is to be toward providing more service, is that gauged by hours of student time volunteered to the community and profession or faculty hours devoted to professional organizations? If you want the department to grow its own resources, does that mean obtaining federal, state, and local dollars through grants and contracts or expanding curriculum to include high-demand degrees?

If you are having trouble clarifying the focus of your administration, you might try an exercise that is used with dissertation and thesis students: *express the themes most important to you in twenty-five words or less.* If you are having trouble doing this, keep trying. Once you have captured what you would truly like to accomplish during your tenure as chair, your sense of where you would like to lead the department will become clear.

Understand the Importance of Department Meetings

Department meetings should be held when more can be accomplished in a large group than through individual or small group meetings. Department meetings are the chair's primary venue for the public demonstration of management and leadership competency. Chairs who are organized, who honor the value of the faculty by being efficient in the use of their meeting time to enhance department productivity, and who respect the rights of all faculty (not just the best liked or most admired) can elevate themselves in the eyes of the department.

Always follow an agenda. There are times when decisions can be made and times when further discussion and data gathering are more important. Know when to employ committees to study, recommend, and draft for later review. Knowledge of *Robert's Rules of Order* is necessary but insufficient. Even when the majority carries a vote, there may be so much disagreement that it will lead to inefficiency and hard feelings down the road.

Follow Through

Both department meeting minutes and faculty memories record the will of the faculty and what chairs say they will do. To maintain the confidence of the faculty, as well as to move the department agenda forward, always do what you say you will do.

If it is agreed that a committee will be established to study some issue, form the committee. Let everyone know who is on it, what they are looking at, and the timeline for their final report. If more data are needed or if clarification of some policy or definition will help the faculty, make sure that the requisite information is gathered and provided to the faculty as promised. Credibility comes from saying what you will do and doing what you say you will do.

ESSENTIAL READING BEFORE TAKING OFFICE

No professor would even think about beginning class without being fully prepared, and this usually involves reading and understanding essential literature and data. The same should hold true for faculty about to begin their duties as chief department administrator. Before chairs can do their work, they need to get a sense of their financial, curricular, and legal environments and what they have to work with.

Read, annotate with observations and questions, and try to understand these essential documents. It will probably be necessary to get together with your office manager to learn the nomenclature and histories behind each document. Visiting with those who have previously served as chairs and other trusted administrators will help new chairs understand this most essential material.

Be sure you have read the following before your first day in the department chair's office:

- Department faculty workload report for most recent academic year. This report should describe what each of your faculty did in the way of instruction, scholarship, and service.
- Two financial documents: the department annual budget and the department end-of-year expense summary report. The budget projects how much the department calculates it will need to spend in various expenditure categories in the coming year. The annual end-of-year expense summary describes what was actually spent in those expenditure categories in the past year.
- Course schedules for the previous academic year (make sure the instructor of record and enrollments are reported for each section). This report describes when each section was offered and how many students signed up for each.
- The faculty personnel handbook and, if you are a collective-bargaining campus, your contract manual. These are the most important personnel documents that describe what is expected of faculty and administrators.

CHAPTER SEVEN

PLANNING

Dr. Krakow, the Education Department's only tenured associate professor, is scheduled to occupy the position of department chair in the fall. She has been asked by her dean to plan for changes mandated by the new president and trustees for the institution. She will need two specific plans: a plan for tying the department mission in with the mission of her department's four-year liberal arts college and a new personnel plan to ensure that tenure, promotion, and retention reviews employ criteria most relevant to the institution's new mission emphases.

While trying to plan her own coursework for the year, she is scrambling to determine where to begin. She knows she doesn't want to go it alone, but she's uncertain whom she needs to include in the planning process. And she has no idea at all what her department mission plan, personnel plan, and resource plan should look like.

She decides to begin at the beginning, by drawing up a tentative timeline for the planning process. She adds dates by which she believes actions will be taken, with measures to be used to determine the outcome of the planning process at each stage. Then she wonders, "What next?"

Dr. Krakow's idea to begin at the beginning seemed like a logical plan, but it soon left her walking in circles. Before chairs can move a department forward, they need to know where to go. Stephen Covey (2004, p. 95) puts it succinctly: "Begin with the end in mind." In other words, effective chair leadership begins with a clear sense of what your department's best work should look like and feel like, how the department should operate, and how the department fits into the overall organization.

Planning can benefit your department in a number of ways:

- It can lead to positive outcomes for the department.
- It can gain commitment from the individuals involved in study and support for their recommendations for action.
- It can provide the opportunity for coalitions to form in support of certain positions.
- It can delay or defer certain actions or positions that are not in the interests of the department.

As noted, there are two parts to effective planning: vision planning and strategy. The vision is your destination, where you want the department to end up. The strategy is how you're going to get there—like plotting a route on a map. Inevitably, you will encounter detours, delays, and hazards along the way; and unanticipated events may make you reconsider your route. Even the best plans need to be reviewed along the way.

CREATING A VISION FOR THE FUTURE

It's easy for new chairs to get overwhelmed quickly if they begin by trying to deal with every problem and issue that hits their desk. It's much better—for the chair's peace of mind and the smooth running of the department—to begin by formulating a vision for the goals you'd like the department to meet during your tenure as chair. To develop a department vision, first take some time to understand where your department stands in terms of curriculum, faculty, funding, classes, and so on, and then formulate a vision of each of these elements for the future. As you do, consider the following topic areas.

What Makes Your Department Distinctive?

Every department needs an identity that distinguishes it from the pack and draws students and financial support to the school. For example, Dr. Jones led the Social Work Department at a university with close military ties. He envisioned a department that would be of particular benefit to a service region filled with military bases, businesses that support the military, hospitals that serve veterans, and dependents educated in local public schools. To implement his vision, he developed a degree in licensed clinical social work aimed at preparing graduates to work with veterans and their families. Such a program fits within the service mission of the public university, has a ready pool of new students, and distinguishes the department from the many other social work departments in the state and nation. New faculty recruited for this Department of Social Work are especially attractive if they have experience working with military populations, funding connections to the Department of Veterans Affairs, and experience teaching veterans and active military.

What areas should your department be invested in? Don't just pick one out of the air; take a hard look at your environment and resources, as Dr. Jones did. Then develop a plan to strengthen your distinctive program areas and empower key faculty who will distinguish your department.

Cui bono: *Who Stands to Gain?*

All processes in which the department engages should contribute primarily toward meeting the needs of the unit's primary beneficiary. For example, Dr. Bacic, a Math Department chair, looked at his math curriculum and found a number of low-enrollment sections. When he looked into these further, he discovered that too many of the sections were built around curriculum that had been designed to favor a particular professor's scholarly interest rather than around courses that students needed to prepare them for advanced curriculum in the sciences, engineering, and computer design—newly popular majors requiring math support.

Dr. Bacic took his question— *"Cui bono?"*—to the faculty, who agreed that the students must always come first. They also agreed that the department should make room in faculty workloads for math courses needed by large numbers of students in the sciences, engineering, and computer design and to teach their own favorite courses once every other year.

Who is your department's primary beneficiary? Is it students, faculty, administration, community, alumni, business partners, or other constituents? Of these, who has the greatest need or the most to contribute?

What Are Your Core Programs?

New chairs should be certain that they understand which programs can really be termed core programs. It may not be the ones everyone assumes.

Department curriculum is sometimes the result of the accretion of faculty interests over the years. Courses and curriculum are often designed in response to faculty interests, and those courses and curriculum may continue to be expressed in course schedules and workloads even as social and occupational needs change and even after the faculty member for whom that curriculum was designed ceases to be a member of the department. The chair has the authority and a broad enough view of the curriculum and schedule to adjust department course offerings so as to maintain centrality to the core mission of the unit.

To get started determining a department's curricular core, list all of your programs: majors, minors, certificates, electives. Rank them from most to least central to fulfilling your department mission. Then ask yourself why you have you ranked them in this way. Would everyone in your department agree? Be sure to consider the following:

- Which program areas for majors are most central?
- Are some elective and general studies areas most critical?
- Where should your department's core faculty be assigned?
- What types of teaching, scholarship, and service should faculty engage that will be most supportive of the department core?
- How many faculty do you need, and in what program areas?

One way to home in on these issues is by "gaming": playing out scenarios as if they were real. Think, what would you do if you were told that you had to plan for a 20 percent one-year budget reduction? This exercise will help you determine what courses, majors, and electives are truly "mission critical" and which are not.

To model out the 20-percent-cut scenario, gather the following information:

- Total department budget and allocations
- Total department expenses divided into major expense categories (including personnel costs)

If the total budget for department operations and personnel came to $1 million, where would you cut if you had to cut 20 percent, or $200,000, from that budget next year? (This level of reduction is drastic but not unprecedented.) After eliminating operational funding for equipment, supplies, phones, travel, and professional development, most departments will still need to find ways to eliminate a hefty chunk of the budget. For most schools, the largest expense category is personnel—and it is there that the remaining reduction would have to be found.

An essential assumption is that the department cannot go into a "death spiral," in which the course schedule and curriculum will not support enough students and the department will lose its ability to fund its own operations. What faculty expertise would be needed to avoid the death spiral? What curriculum would have to be protected in order to continue to deliver the curriculum that attracts majors and elective students? Who teaches those courses as their first, second, or even third teaching area?

In the event of a 20 percent reduction, who can access new and steady resource streams, thereby strengthening the department's resource base? Who can access federal, state, and local grants and contracts? Whose research agenda is robust enough to fund graduate students and faculty in support of that research? Consideration of these and other questions will help department chairs determine who and what are central, less central, and peripheral to the department's core mission.

Who Should Teach What?

Planning allows leaders to move resources where they are most needed. Plan the long-term reapportionment of resources by looking at your nondiscretionary resources. When will they become available for reallocation? Plot out all of your tenured and tenure-track lines by area of specialization. How long will faculty in each area secure that specialization as a viable emphasis in your department? When and where should these resources be reallocated?

What Would Your Ideal Department Look Like?

Envision your ideal department, and engage your faculty in the visioning process. Research other departments on your campus, in your state, and across the nation. When you find some "model" departments, look deeper: Why did you choose these departments?

What specific qualities can your department emulate? Look especially at the following areas:

- *Governance:* What does the department governance structure look like? Does that governance chart look like yours?
- *Faculty compensation:* Is compensation comparable to yours? How much "extra compensation" is permitted over and above salary?
- *Faculty mix:* What is the faculty mix relative to faculty categories of full/associate/assistant professors, tenured/tenure-track/non-tenure-track instructors, term contracts, adjuncts, and teaching associates/assistants? What kinds of research do the faculty conduct?
- *Workload:* How many sections and students are taught per academic year? How much funded research is expected? How much publication is expected?
- *Evaluations:* How are faculty evaluated? How is faculty performance measured or operationalized in regard to teaching, scholarship, and service?
- *Classes and students:* What are the most popular majors? What elective courses do students select, and which are the most popular? What is the mix of undergraduate and graduate students?
- *Budget:* Where does the money go? What percentage of the budget is allocated to professional development? Equipment? Graduate student support? Office and research support?

WRITING A VISION STATEMENT

Once you have thought your vision through, write it down and share it with department faculty. This will help you all understand the department's desired direction, and sharing it will help gain support down the line. Typically, vision statements say something about the department context, the department's primary objectives in its work, and how it intends to reach its most valued goals.

For example, the Department of Physics in a four-year liberal arts college might have a vision statement that looks like this:

The physics program at our college provides an opportunity to study the most fundamental science in an intimate liberal arts environment that emphasizes individual interactions between faculty and students.

In contrast, the Physics Department vision statement for a research university is somewhat different:

> Our undergraduate physics program aims to provide a broad and solid background in fundamental physics through introductory course work and then to engage all our majors who are interested in current research with some of the top research groups world-wide. We aim to help our majors develop strong mathematical and analytical skills, good laboratory skills, effective written and oral communication skills, and a solid understanding of the fundamental laws that govern the universe in preparation for advanced work in physics and its related fields of study, as well as applied professional fields.

The vision statement provides substance for discussions within the department as to the unit's primary objectives, the context in which it operates, and the methods or technology it uses to reach its goals. Consideration of vision statement models by the entire faculty will lead to input that may be refined by a department committee tasked with producing the final department vision statement. All of this helps give an idea to department members about where their work should be directed.

STRATEGIC PLANNING

Once you have your general goals and vision, you can map out a way to get there. As you did with the vision process, engage the faculty's help in formulating new strategies. Get specific. You may have to change the specifics as time goes on, and you see what works, but a clear path is better than one that is nebulous. Plan your strategies in the following areas.

Map Out an Annual Plan for the Department

It is wise to set out the year's objectives in writing and to establish a calendar of department work. Such a proactive plan allows chairs not only to manage their unit but also to lead it to a brighter future. Make sure that your department is active in each of the areas that matter to campus leaders. That is, make sure that there is evidence of good teaching, sufficient scholarship, an appropriate level of funded activity, and high-quality service to campus, the community, and professional organizations.

Strategic planning for your department should seem familiar: it resembles the instructional lesson plan you may make for the courses you teach or a research design that guides scholarly investigation. With a desired goal in mind, map out activities for each month that will support reaching that objective.

For example, if the goal is to "grow revenue streams coming directly to the department," one very positive step in this direction would be to "increase alumni giving." This may call for a series of tasks to be scheduled, such as "grow alumni database," "develop e-newsletter with department and alumni news," "plan alumni reunion," "send out a save-the-date announcement," "form reunion committee," "plan speakers, VIPs, program," and "stage reunion," followed by an appeal for support from alumni earmarked to the department.

Map Out an Annual Plan for Your Faculty

For each of your key faculty, develop an action plan for what the person should accomplish each year. Make sure that each goal is achievable and has sufficient resources to be feasible. Provide operational indicators for each objective. The action plans for individual faculty should together contribute to the achievement of the department's annual goals and work plans.

For faculty who are already strong in teaching and service but who could use support for their research, the annual work plan might include a presentation at a relevant national convention. To actualize a faculty annual plan, establish goals along with the dates by which each step will be completed. Steps should be posted on the calendar. These might include "target professional association meeting and possible publication venues," "form mentoring committee," "draft presentation proposal," "submit proposal," "reserve travel funds," "present proposal," "redraft presentation into publication," and "submit publication." An annual plan for work such as this makes it very clear what is expected of faculty as they seek to improve their performance.

For faculty who could benefit from improved use of technology in their teaching, an annual plan would have dates for steps such as "attend campus IT seminars fall term," "attend Educause annual meeting and report to chair on promising technological applications for the campus," "assign technologically capable graduate assistant to the faculty," "redraft one course to include lesson plans leveraging technological applications," "teach revised course spring term," and "evaluate technologically enhanced course end of spring term."

Map Out an Annual Plan for Yourself

It's important to include yourself in the overall plan and to specify your own goals and strategy: What do you want to accomplish with each faculty member? With your major students? In your curriculum? In your course schedule? In budget management and oversight? In resource generation? In your work with internal and external constituents?

Once you've thought out these goals, plan your strategies. And be sure to put measures in place that will let you know that you are making progress in each area.

Make a Short List of Annual Goals

Make a short list of your most important two or three goals or themes for the year, and keep it in front of you. For example, "Support for grants and contract proposals," "Enhance budget allocation transparency," and "Increase funds for graduate student support by 20 percent" may be key goals for the year. Keep this short list where you can see it, perhaps on your computer screen or on your desk. This list can serve as a keel to keep you sailing in the right direction.

Link Plans

Link annual plans for faculty and the department with other relevant college and institutional plans. Every school has strategic plans. Some plans are abstract; others include operational measures to indicate whether the institution is moving in the right direction. Tie in department plans with other institutional plans and measures.

REACHING FOR CONSENSUS

It is the nature of the academy for vigorous discussion and consideration of multiple views to precede general consensus. Both logic and passion are important parts of what we do.

Chairs can lead discussions within the department to help the unit move toward consensus. Be realistic. Although it may be difficult to get everyone to agree on, say, the exact curriculum content for majors to learn, it may be sufficient to achieve general agreement about the direction to take. For example, the members of a History Department curriculum committee may not agree on the exact texts to incorporate, but they can agree that more multicultural sources should be incorporated.

CHAPTER EIGHT

BUDGET, RESOURCE MANAGEMENT, AND DEVELOPMENT

Dr. Clark is in his first year as chair of the Art Department. He was expecting a budget cut but not the latest news—a 30 percent reduction to take place over two years. Other units in the College of Arts and Sciences had received reduction targets as low as 5 percent, so his news was especially upsetting—but perhaps not surprising. The department only has about ten majors, and the previous chair didn't manage the budget carefully. When the dean asked why he paid so little attention to fiscal matters, the chair said, "I did not get into higher education to be a bean counter." All of Dr. Clark's faculty—six tenure-track faculty and a host of adjuncts—are members of the union, with a strict order of layoff based on seniority contractually established. Art has primarily been a service department, with most of its enrollments coming from general education and elective students. Dr. Clark needs to draft a plan for his meeting with the dean as soon as possible.

Gone are the days when schools can expect to be given the resources that they say they need. So it is becoming increasingly important for chairs to take the lead to ensure that their departments maximize available resources and invest those resources wisely. These resources include much more than the budget allocated to the department.

Budgets detail the dollars spent to operate the department over the fiscal year. But the resources available to the chair include much more. Resources include your faculty workload, as assigned by the chair; faculty achievements, such as their research and service to the institution's friends and service region; student enrollments, which usually vary in value relative to course level; department curriculum; class schedule every term; alumni; community and business partners; special programs and events; and your department's good name.

Managing department resources ensures that *all* of the assets available to the department will be used efficiently. By developing their department's resource streams, chairs can enlarge the assets that may be invested in the department's good works. In other words, "margin" makes possible the achievement of "mission."

INCOME AND EXPENSES

Before you can manage your budget, you need to know what you have to work with. For this task, your budget manager is your first resource. Make the following requests of your budget manager:

Please provide me with an overview of all income and assets for the department and individual faculty.

Please provide me with an overview of all expenses and debts and liabilities for the department and individual faculty.

Your total department income and expenses and assets and liabilities should be summarized on one or two spreadsheet pages.

Income includes the annual department allocations to cover normal operating expenses such as personnel. It may also include income from grant and contract residuals; "premiums," or extra charges that come to the department for high-demand programs; rent and lease income that may come to the department from fees charged for use of its space or equipment; and other income, such as funds accrued in accounts that are in the name of faculty and not under direct control of the chair.

Expenses and liabilities charged to the department and its faculty include personnel charges (broken down by tenure-track, non-tenure-track, full-time and part-time non-tenure-track, graduate teaching and research assistants, student workers, staff); benefits; equipment purchases and leases; maintenance contracts; space rentals; and deferred expenses (long-term payouts on debt).

Sweeps and Carryforwards

Most academic fiscal years run from July 1 of the current year to June 30 of the following year. Find out if you are permitted to roll over or carry forward funds from one fiscal year to the next. Are faculty permitted to carry into the next fiscal year their own funds earned from grants and contracts? Department chairs are much more likely to seek economies and to enhance resources if they are allowed by their institutional policies and officers to move unexpended money into the next fiscal year.

How often have we seen administrators hurriedly spend on just about anything to avoid the end-of-the-year loss of money remaining in their accounts (the dreaded "sweep"), when higher-level administration returns funds remaining in department accounts to its own centralized accounts. For example, if a department's copying allocation was $5,000 but the department expended only $2,000 during the fiscal year, the remaining $3,000 is "swept" out of the department's account and returned to the central administration's accounts. If, by contrast, chairs and department faculty are permitted to carry funds forward and to accumulate resources they have earned so that they will have sufficient funds for investment in their own research, programs, and students, this is a strong positive incentive to be financially prudent and entrepreneurial in their approach to resource production.

Find out if your campus policies permit department carryforward and if they permit individual faculty carryforward of research funds. Perhaps your dean will "officially" sweep your funds at the end of the fiscal year but guarantee that those funds or a percentage of those funds will be allocated to you at the beginning of the next fiscal year.

Expenditure Accounting

With the help of your budget manager, analyze your department end-of-year expenditure report. Which expenses are fixed and which are discretionary? Tenured faculty salaries are fixed, but can any fixed expenses be modified so that they become "unfixed"?

For example, are all of the dollars used last year for part-time instruction required again this year? Can sections be combined or offered once a year instead of every term? Can other courses (either within or outside of the department) satisfy major requirements? Do all electives have to be offered as frequently?

If personnel expenses for just two or three sections can be saved and reallocated to the operational budget, what had been seen as "fixed expenses" may be freed to become part of the operational budget. Freeing the adjunct expenses of three sections, for example, may add significantly to funds available for professional development, student workers, or graduate students.

Discretionary Dollars

It is a rule of thumb in business management to plan for a reserve account equal to 2 to 5 percent of the organization's total budget. For a department of ten full-time faculty, it is not unusual for the entire budget for personnel and operating costs to total about $1 million. Following this rule of thumb, chairs should have a reserve account of between $20,000 and $50,000. To the business manager for a private for-profit business, these funds would be reserved as a "rainy day" fund available for unforeseen expenses. In institutions of higher education, however, expenses tend to be much more predictable because there are two or three primary periods during the academic year when equipment and supplies will be purchased, and enrollments will determine expenditures. By carefully monitoring the rate of expenditures, and armed with knowledge as to when department dollars are expended (for example, most equipment purchases occur at the beginning of the fiscal year), the "reserve account" becomes a "discretionary account" that can be invested in the department's future.

Where can those discretionary dollars be directed to have the most impact? Do your allocations match your department priorities? What can you do to help match up priorities with expenditures now and in the future?

ALUMNI RESOURCES

Dr. Hassan is fortunate that his Department of Computer Engineering (CE) has more support than most other departments in the university. On the board of trustees (BOT) is a graduate of CE who is being groomed to take over as chair of the BOT next year. Furthermore, a number of potential major donors are being courted by the Office of Advancement. They have already given in the $50,000 range and are seen as future donors in the $250,000 range. Dr. Hassan knows that his department's greatest asset is the excellent preparation his students receive. He also knows, however, that it never hurts to have friends who are well positioned with university leadership.

Your alumni can be among your most valuable resources. Work with your alumni office to cultivate them—not only for major gifts but also for annual fund contributions. Ask your alumni office what percentage of your majors contribute to the department. Even an extra $10 per year from an additional 2 percent of your alumni can mean a significant increase in this important recurring discretionary fund available for chair allocation.

Annual fund contributions can really add up. An average of forty majors graduating each year over an institution's fifty-year history means that there are two thousand alumni for that department. If 20 percent contribute $25 each year, this will benefit the department by $10,000 annually. Depending on your local and state protocols, those annual fund dollars may be the most discretionary funds you have, available for expenses ranging from student scholarships and travel funds to the payment of food and beverage costs for department events.

Fundraising and "Friendmaking"

Enlarge your alumni donations to the annual fund by increasing the percentage of your majors who contribute and the amount that they contribute. Appoint a faculty member, staff, or some of your best students to work on these fundraising efforts. Hire your major students, or perhaps public relations majors or marketing majors, to call alumni to reestablish friendships and to bolster the annual fund. It's amazing what pizza can do to boost the connections with alumni made by your best majors at the campus call center.

You can also use social media, such as Facebook and LinkedIn, to engage your alumni. "Friendmaking" always precedes "fundraising." Alumni who give tend to continue giving. What they give tends to increase as they earn more.

Earmarked Alumni Donations

Find out whether your alumni direct their contributions to the institution or to the department or if they do not specify. Undirected contributions will typically go toward your institution's general alumni fund instead of your department account.

Contributions directed to the department may be more beneficial for your faculty and students, especially if these are unrestricted funds that can be used at the discretion of the chair for support of department operations. Do all you can to ensure that your alumni contributions go to the department, and include this information in your fundraising efforts.

PERSONNEL RESOURCES

Personnel are the department's biggest resource, whether your department has just a few or as many as fifty full-time faculty members. It is the faculty who teach students and bring the enrollment that is the lifeblood for most colleges and universities. Faculty also bring in external funding and do the meaningful work that engenders connections with the community, government, business, and other friends of the institution.

Position Control and Dollar Control Management

For most institutions, personnel costs are the single biggest annual expense. In some institutions, personnel costs are managed through what is known as position control, in others through dollar control. In *position control,* a certain number of full-time positions are allocated to departments. The accounting and management of the dollars associated with each position is done usually at the dean's office. In a department that has five full-time tenure-track faculty (typically expressed as five full-time-equivalent faculty, or 5 FTEF) and four half-time faculty (4 times $\frac{1}{2}$ equals 2 FTEF), the department would therefore have a total of 7 FTEF. Although the total personnel budget for a department this size could equal $600,000 annually, dollars for salaries and benefits are managed centrally at the dean's office under this management system used. Chairs and department staff do not need to account for or manage dollars in position control systems.

In *dollar control* management, the department is allocated a certain number of dollars to spend as it sees fit, so long as the dean's office approves. If the department's total personnel allocation is $600,000 annually, it is the responsibility of the chair and office staff to account for and manage the use of this money. All faculty expenditures must come from the $600,000. This includes expense for tenured, tenure-earning, and non-tenure-track full-time and part-time faculty. With dollar control, the dean's office manages from a greater distance, keeping an overall eye on expenditures while leaving regular management and decision making to the department.

Spending Personnel Dollars

Whatever the personnel management system that is used, it is important for chairs to try to maximize the benefits that may come from wise use of personnel dollars. Does their expense justify their cost? Does the department's productivity justify the institution's expenditure? Or should personnel resources be reallocated into other institutional units?

Is your department currently maximizing the benefits that should come from your personnel dollars? To determine if personnel dollars are well spent, administrators will typically look at student enrollment first. How many elective and major students are registered for courses in the department?

Meeting Enrollment Targets

Some departments are given a target enrollment number for each academic term. If your department needs to meet target enrollment numbers, how is that target measured? Is it headcount or FTES (full-time-equivalent students)? Is it the measurement the same for undergraduate and graduate enrollments? Once you have these enrollment numbers, look at your faculty numbers. What personnel are required to staff the classes needed to meet that enrollment target? What personnel are you now employing? Do you need all of that personnel expense?

If department personnel are managed with a dollar control system, it may be possible—with careful scheduling and workload assignments—for chairs to carve out portions of the personnel budget that are not required to pay for class instruction and support. This gives chairs have an opportunity to invest in other parts of the department.

Reallocating Personnel Dollars

It's likely that most of your department money is in personnel. Ask your dean if you have permission to reallocate dollars saved from your department personnel budget toward other faculty and student needs (so long as instructional requirements are met, of course). To illustrate the power of reallocated personnel dollars, consider the following scenario.

One of your faculty, Professor Smith, has asked to take an unpaid halftime leave, thereby releasing $30,000 from his $60,000 annual salary. Two part-time faculty, paid $5,000 per class, are each assigned to cover one section each of Professor Smith's normal teaching load. This nets the department $20,000 for other faculty, staff, and student needs.

See if you can carve out $300 to $500 chunks of money from possible department expenditures that can be deferred, reduced, or canceled. Invest each amount for professional development or for targeted projects.

NEW RESOURCE STREAMS

Onetime allocations are nice. But revenue streams that the department can count on for needed funds are better because they continue through the years. These revenue streams include contracts, grants, target enrollments that come with resources, executive degree programs, publications, workshops, and conferences sponsored by your department.

As chair of an academic department, you have the power and influence to initiate meetings with public and private organizations that may need services for which they are glad to pay. Take advantage of your position to bring money into your department for years to come.

Contracts

Contracts for services may be renewed year after year. They are a great way to pay students and provide the scholarly experience and professional contacts that may lead to jobs after they graduate.

Grants and contracts usually bring a residual return to the principal investigator and to the department, college, and university. These residuals can be invested in future research and funded proposals. A $100,000 annual contract, for example, may yield anywhere from 0 percent to over 50 percent "indirect return," depending on the source of the funding and restrictions on indirect return. That indirect return is then allocated to the campus offices and individuals according to institutional protocols.

As department chair, you can serve as a liaison between contract organizations and the faculty able to provide services. Remember, you are no longer merely faculty; when you call to set up an appointment to discuss mutual interests and collaborative opportunities, those organizations will be especially attentive to your request.

Grants

Grants are usually for specific projects with start and end dates. Enlist your research office to help you keep on the lookout for requests for proposals for your faculty. Improve grant prospects by hiring experienced grant writers to draft proposals. Cultivate funding agencies by helping your faculty get to know directors of programs who solicit proposals in areas where your faculty have expertise. Support your faculty by encouraging them to attend meetings where they will meet potential principal investigators and program officers. Get copies of successful proposals on which your faculty may model new proposals.

Successful grants typically return to departments a portion of indirect funds, but they are often accompanied by money to pay for administration and teaching buyouts, usually at the lead faculty member's rate of pay. If a professor's rate of pay is $10,000 per course for a two-course buyout totaling $20,000, and if adjunct replacement faculty may be paid at a rate of $5,000 per course for total replacement cost of $10,000, the net return to the department is $10,000 over and above the cost of hiring instructional replacements. An additional $10,000 thus becomes available for allocation toward the department's other needs.

Grant success takes at least as much persistence as intelligence. Let your faculty know that every grant proposal is a learning experience that better prepares them for the next draft submission. It is also heartening to know that proposals may be regarded favorably in the course of annual performance reviews, should that be the case at your institution.

Resource-Generating Enrollments

Not all enrollments are equal. Some enrollments are greater in the value that they bring to the institution and the department. Tuition and fees may vary with the major degree. Graduate enrollments are usually funded at a higher rate than undergraduate enrollments for public schools. Some degree programs and nondegree certificate programs earn a premium for their schools—that is, they charge an extra fee that can be divided among the institution, department, faculty, and staff involved.

Revenue Earners

Look into developing revenue earners such as executive degree programs and nondegree certificate programs. Look, too, into developing programs that work within the career restrictions of adult learners. Are there managers in your community who want to earn advanced degrees so that they can move up? Are there working professionals such as nurses or teachers who need continuing education units but can pursue those units only on weekends, in summer, or in the evening? Should all or part of these classes be offered online asynchronously—that is, accessible when students have the time to log into the class that is maintained on a server—to make it possible for working adults to enroll in your programs?

Executive programs can sometimes charge a premium over and above normal tuition. Tuition for these programs will sometimes be paid by the employer since advanced training can benefit a company, school, hospital, or industry.

Manuals, Workbooks, and Readers

Consider the creation of manuals, workbooks, and readers. Look into the feasibility of using customized manuals, workbooks, and readers that have been created for students taking your classes. Sometimes these self-produced works can substitute for much more expensive commercially produced textbooks, readers, or lab manuals.

Can you pay advanced students to draft manuals or workbooks under the direction of the instructional faculty? After ensuring copyright compliance, editing, and revision, these self-produced works may be sold through your campus bookstore, with proceeds paying for student labor, production costs, and bookstore fees. The remainder can go into faculty seed accounts to be invested in student workers, faculty research, or professional development. Self-produced manuals, workbooks, and readers can save students 50 percent or more on their book costs, help pay students for their work, and also serve as an independent source of faculty development funds.

SPECIAL EVENTS, ANNUAL CONFERENCES, AND WORKSHOPS

The good name and professional contacts of the department and the institution may be leveraged to provide events of value to professionals, the community, alumni, and institutional friends. Such events may be revenue sources for the departments that sponsor, host, and work these events.

Summer Projects

Look at summer as a source of revenue. Are you making best use of the summer for resource generation? For faculty scholarship? If summers are not typically devoted to a full load of institutionally supported instruction, what are the faculty doing during this time? What can be done to make greater use of the summertime to benefit your students, faculty, and department?

Special-Session Courses

Does your department offer intersession courses? Can special-session courses be offered? Often students need to catch up or want to get ahead. Courses may be filled during regular sessions, or students may need to retake courses for a higher grade or just to make sure they understand the material.

Intersession may exist already as an official calendar period, when courses may be offered apart from fall, spring, and summer terms. Or intersession may be created between any calendar periods during which your institution already offers courses. By using the calendar efficiently, additional course sections may be offered, annual enrollments may be increased, tuition and fees may be collected, faculty may earn extra income, and students may have a wider selection of courses to choose from.

FACULTY INCENTIVES

Faculty incentives might include money, assigned time, travel funding, equipment, or student labor. What does it take to incentivize faculty to do what the department, students, and constituents need done? The potential incentives discussed here include extra compensation, research accounts, funded research and indirect aid available from this work, and internal sabbaticals.

Extra Compensation

Before you make any plans, find out what the campus legal maximum is for extra compensation. It may be 25 percent over and above annual salary, but it could be more or less depending on your state, institution, and legal exceptions.

Research Seed Accounts

Find out what the campus rules are for research seed accounts. Funds that come from grants or contracts typically have a percentage set aside that goes directly to the primary investigator's (PI's) research account. This amount is over and above what the PI is paid for labor that may take place during the summer or during some other noninstitutional employment period. It may be more beneficial to stock a research seed account that is not taxed than to pay a faculty member to be a PI.

Spurs to Faculty Participation

Does your institution have an up-to-date list of funded projects, dollar amounts, and primary investigators? Sometimes when faculty see a list of their colleagues who have been successful, it is enough to trigger their competitive instincts and get them moving on a project they may have been putting off for years.

Sometimes faculty feel that the amount of work involved is not enough to justify the small return. Find out how the rate of return is determined, by which faculty and your department receive indirect return as principal investigators for research grants and contracts. If the amount strikes you as low, talk to research administrators about enhancing the rate of return so that your faculty have greater incentive to do this kind of work.

Internal Sabbaticals

Consider initiating "internal sabbaticals." Most schools have sabbaticals for their faculty, but funding for these has been reduced due to tight budgets. So long as your department serves the needs of its majors and other majors and meets its historical enrollment levels, it may be possible to create a program whereby faculty teach a bit more during some terms so that they can self-fund sabbaticals within the department.

For example, a faculty member who is willing and able to teach an extra section in some area that the department needs can then bank those credits toward an internal sabbatical. This benefits the department as well as the faculty member.

Student Help

Sometimes our most talented faculty are so busy teaching or coordinating department programs that they are unable to leverage their talents and network to enhance some revenue stream. Your most important resource is faculty. Sometimes the assignment of advanced senior or graduate students to help faculty with the routine chores of instruction and grading may more than pay for this minor personnel cost by freeing up talented faculty to pursue external funding or to pursue some other program with revenue potential.

Determine which faculty could most benefit from more student help. Whose teaching, scholarship, or service could benefit from the assignment of either advanced students or graduate students to support them?

You, too, can benefit from student help. For example, management of department financial affairs includes the supervision of department expenses. One of the largest expenses for your students is books. Having a student add up the cost of books and materials for each course your department offers can aid you enormously. Ask one of your majors to develop an accounting summary of books and other materials assigned by your faculty for their classes. Classify each such cost as "required" or "optional." After completion of the text accounting summary, determine with each faculty member if these costs can be reduced while maintaining course quality. Especially for public colleges and universities with tuition in the $5,000-per-year range, books can easily add another 20 percent to that amount.

MISCELLANEOUS COST-CUTTING MEASURES

Once you start looking, you'll begin to find cost-cutting measures everywhere. For example, does your department still need landline phones? This is a small question with potentially large repercussions in dollars spent. For example, if a ten-member department has thirty phones and each phone costs the department $10 per month, this adds up to $3,600 per year. If faculty and staff are using cell phones and e-mail most of the time, these phones may be superfluous.

Have a student worker check to see if phone numbers are being used in the rooms assigned to your faculty and staff. Are all the phone numbers and monthly bills that are charged against your department actually being used? If you do discover unused or minimally used phones, find out before you disconnect them whether, if you save those funds, you will be able to apply the allocation toward some other department need.

Another area to look at is your department's "financial entitlement." Some institutions employ a funding formula to determine financial entitlement. Such formulas are typically based on variables such as number of students; how many credits they complete; the level of the courses they complete (introductory, advanced, master's, doctoral); and whether the course is presented in lecture, lab, research, or thesis or dissertation mode. Is your department receiving what it is entitled to? If you adjust your enrollments to earn higher entitlements, will your department receive a larger allocation?

MAKING YOUR BUDGET PUBLIC

Transparency goes a long way toward building goodwill. Once you have developed your department budget, share it. Put it online (omitting confidential information, of course) so that everyone can see it.

Department Budget Meeting

Hold a department meeting to review the budget, allocations, and expense histories. Be sure to specify and define how much department money is nondiscretionary versus discretionary, encumbered, or owed and how much is tied up in personnel in each of its tenure-track, non-tenure-track, full-time, and part-time categories.

Depending on the points you want to make, you may also want to display cost per enrollment at various class levels, how much is available for travel and professional development, how much is earned in the way of grants and contracts, and how much is spent on student help and staffing.

Use graphic displays to get your points across. Historical trend data will give faculty a sense of the direction for expenditures, allocation, and income.

Budget Calendar

Make a budget calendar showing the dates when draft budgets are to be received by each particular office. Include the names of each budget officer and when draft budgets are scheduled to go to the next level. Then print out the calendar, post it, and put it online.

CHAPTER NINE

CURRICULUM, SCHEDULING, AND INSTRUCTION

Dr. Brown has just been appointed chair of the Department of Agriculture at a medium-size comprehensive state university. She was hired from outside of the university, and although she enjoys the dean's support, she is uncertain of the level of support she has among the department's faculty. Surveying department enrollments, she sees that some sections are sparsely populated, almost all classes are offered from 9:00 A.M. to 3:00 P.M. on Mondays and Wednesdays or Tuesdays and Thursdays, and three of the department's four major degree programs have fewer than five declared majors in each. Her dean tells her that unlike other departments in the College of Science, Agriculture has almost no external funding. The former chair of the department is the incoming chair of the faculty senate. He is not in favor of online courses, and in response to student calls for hybrid courses, he remarked, "That is not why I was hired here."

The dean has called for curriculum reform, instructional innovation, and responsiveness to student needs, and Dr. Brown feels the weight of her responsibilities from day one. She hopes she can do something to help Agriculture, but the problems seem overwhelming. How should she even begin to sort things out?

Higher education's coin of the realm is ideas. For comprehensive universities, baccalaureate colleges, and two-year institutions, the preponderance of a department's resources are expended and earned through its curriculum, scheduling, and instruction. As department chair, it's your job to see to their smooth running

and benefit for the department and its students. After consideration, for example, you may find yourself adding new, innovative
programs and courses to the schedule, or you may find that you
need to prune the curriculum and course schedule to strengthen
them. The suggestions in this chapter should prove useful for
maximizing the impact of these vital aspects of student learning.

CURRICULUM

A department's curriculum is the expression of the most important ideas in the disciplines and professions that are managed in
that department. As faculty, you are likely familiar with the curriculum currently being offered and have your own ideas on possible
changes and innovations. As chair, with responsibility for curriculum, you may find that you have a broader perspective and a new
interest in refreshing this area. The following suggestions can help
you understand this fundamental departmental responsibility.

New Programs

Look around the country at departments you admire to discover
good programs they may have that your institution does not offer.

Talk with the people and organizations that employ your
majors and that you serve. What new programs do your constituents need?

Research the feasibility of adding those needed programs.
What faculty could be retrained and retasked? When could new
hires be made? What timeline could work?

To accelerate program development, pay faculty (or emeritus
faculty) to create new needed curriculum to be made available to
the department for consideration.

General Education Courses

General education or general studies courses will help you meet
your enrollment targets and recruit students into your major. Do
you have enough general education and general studies courses,
and enough sections of those courses, to provide you with enrollment flexibility?

Put Your Best Face on General Ed Courses. As your most public
face, your department's general education courses affect the most

students. The faculty who teach these courses are representing your department to the public. Think about who is teaching these introductory and general education courses. Are they primarily new faculty or faculty who really don't want to teach those courses? How many of those sections are taught by your best faculty?

Schedule Only What You Need. By scheduling only what you need, your department will either save money or free faculty for other assignments.

Are there courses in other departments that will substitute for any of your major course requirements? To save faculty time and department money, do you want to take turns offering the course if it will serve both departments' majors?

Faculty will always have their favorite specialized courses to teach. Over time, however, those courses build up and may be maintained even after the faculty member leaves the department. But student and social needs change over time, without regard for these old favorites. Can you offer nonessential courses less regularly—say, every other year or every three or four years?

SCHEDULING

The department's course schedule describes how often, when, and by whom the curriculum is offered. Well-constructed schedules benefit students, who can more easily enroll in needed courses; the faculty who teach them; and the department as a whole.

Consider Target Enrollment Numbers

If your department has a target enrollment number, it's important to understand whether this is measured by number of students or by some kind of weighted teaching unit based on numbers of students, level of coursework, and mode of instruction. You will also need to know if it is the same for undergraduate and graduate courses.

If you can deviate from the enrollment target without penalty, find out if there is a limit to this deviation. How many sections can you prune without penalty? This can have a direct positive impact on your department budget. For example, each adjunct section saved can be $2,000 to $5,000 that you may be able to reallocate toward professional development, student help, or other department needs. Every section that one of your full-time faculty does not have to teach may be redirected toward scholarship, service, curriculum development, improving their teaching, or other department needs.

Construct a Longitudinal Schedule History

Develop a spreadsheet that gives you a different look at your courses and class schedule. In the left-hand column, list all of your courses. Across the tops of the remaining columns, list every academic term in which courses have been offered over the past several years. In each cell, list the number of sections of each course that have been offered over the past three years' terms. If you would like more detail, list the percentage of maximum enrollment for each cell.

This spreadsheet will quickly give you and your department a good idea as to what has been offered, how much, and how close to capacity each section has been filled. Then you can discuss what needs to change and what can stay the same.

Encourage Even Little Bits of Enrollment

Any business manager who can quickly add 5 percent to the unit's bottom line is seen as a genius. How would you like an additional 5 to 10 percent added to your personal resources?

Here's one way to it. In sections with prior maximum enrollment of twenty, if you add one student to one more seat, you have increased capacity, enrollment, and perhaps resource entitlement by 5 percent. Add two students in two seats, and you have increased this resource by 10 percent.

Are there courses that warrant and would benefit from being one extra unit or being one extra unit as an option for more work, additional assignments, or service? Courses for which experiential credit or an extra-credit research project may be assigned can easily bolster your enrollments while also awarding course credit for the extra work that students are doing.

Are students who do research for faculty receiving academic credit for this work? It might benefit your department enrollments to offer them independent study credit or to mass all students doing research in your department into a one-section research course.

Develop a list of internships and other student work experiences in the community, including business partners. Check to see if students are receiving appropriate academic credit for their work. Not only may this help your enrollments, but it will also recognize student experiences with academic credit.

Review the Draft Course Schedule

After you have drafted your course schedule, take time to review it. Consider how well it actually reflects the department priorities in your vision statement. You may be surprised to find that some changes are needed. For example, if a program is the third department priority but it is consuming 50 percent of faculty and operational resources, you should consider adjusting the schedule.

Schedule Classes When Students Can Take Them

The easiest way to look at your schedule is to construct a bar graph that shows the number of classes offered by your department over the course of the seven-day, twenty-four-hour week. This will give you a very clear idea of where changes need to be made.

Are your classes where they belong? Are they distributed throughout the day and week, or are they bunched up during a small number of hours and days? For example, it's not uncommon for most of a department's course sections to be offered on Monday and Wednesday or Tuesday and Thursday between 9:00 A.M. and 5:00 P.M. In the days of full-time students, this made sense. But today, when so many students are juggling work and school, they may not be able work these courses into their schedules.

Are your classes that have a logical sequence offered conveniently for students to take more than one class each time they come to campus? For example, is your research methods class held just before or after the associated math or statistics class?

Consider also whether your department is competing with itself by scheduling its most popular classes in the same time slots or competing with popular courses in other departments that are scheduled at the same times. Free up your students and increase your enrollment by considering weekend and evening classes or new time slots during the week.

Be Aware of Choke Courses

Do you have enough sections of critical courses so that student progress is not blocked by choke courses? Most majors have a few courses that are so crucial to the remaining course of study that they serve as choke courses—that is, progress cannot be made until students pass those courses. Make sure you have enough sections of these courses so that you are not artificially slowing down time to graduation.

Check Classroom Assignments

Sometimes policy will determine the classrooms made available to departments, but often it's just a continuation of what was done last term and the term before that. Often nothing other than past practice determines to which department rooms are given as priority. Are there "better" rooms that you would like and can gain access to? Are there larger rooms that will allow courses to have larger enrollments? Are there rooms that will allow face-to-face instruction with simultaneous digital broadcast capacity?

If you find that your courses would benefit from different classrooms, check other department course schedules to see what is being used. You may find suitable empty classrooms at the times you need them or be able to negotiate a trade.

Consider Jumbo Sections

Will "jumbo sections" work for your curriculum and instruction? What does the pedagogical research say about instructional effectiveness and learning outcomes in your curriculum? If research shows that students learn as much in a section of one hundred as they do in a section of fifty, combining enrollments into larger sections saves faculty time. Having just a few jumbo sections allows departments to maintain more intimate class sizes for the rest of its courses.

If jumbo classrooms are justified but no rooms with larger capacities are available, consider the use of technology. You may be able to connect two rooms via video. Faculty can spend face-to-face time in each room while broadcasting to the other.

Consider Faculty Needs

Scheduling can also have an impact on instructors. For example, do your faculty who need research support have the blocks of time they need to do their scholarship? Ask them what would be their optimal time to do their research that still meets department instructional needs.

INSTRUCTION

Curriculum is conveyed to students through instruction. Issues concerned with instruction can affect your faculty and students in ways you already know as well as in areas you may not have considered.

Decrease Time to Graduation for Your Majors

Students who have to take the same course over again will take away seats that new students need. This may inadvertently and unnecessarily increase the cost of your major to your students, your department, and your institution. For example, just three students retaking a class with an enrollment maximum of thirty are consuming 10 percent of the section's resources. This is especially bad for your enrollments if your department is not credited for students repeating the same course.

Review Class Maximums

How close to class maximums are enrollments? Are there pedagogically defensible reasons or research reasons for listed class maximums? Review courses to see if there are any in which caps be raised.

Consider developing a course that can have large enrollments in one section but can be offered with larger or smaller class maximums so as to be able to "dial up" or "dial down" enrollments for any one term.

Optimize Instructional Modes

Technology has brought new class modalities to education. Review your schedule with regard to whether it has the best mix of face-to-face, online, and blended course delivery modes to meet the needs of your students and faculty. Are your online course offerings appropriately synchronous or asynchronous? Review your sections for the appropriateness of their instructional mode.

Give Your Majors Help in Key Courses

Are you providing enough assistance to students who are doing fine in your other major courses but having difficulty with required "choke" courses? Consider using teaching assistants, technology, or other innovations to help guide them.

Look at Overload Possibilities

Is it in your department's favor to pay your full-time faculty to teach course overloads, or would it be better to pay for part-time faculty? Although part-timers can teach a variety of courses, it is typically the more senior terminal-degreed faculty who can do more advanced courses required for program completion and graduate programs.

Define Graduation Plans

If your department is in a baccalaureate-granting institutions, develop graduation plans for junior college transfers who come in with their first two years of coursework completed and a four-year-major plan for students who began their college careers as freshman in your institution for graduation from your department. Clearly define what courses are required (and which are options as electives) for completion of bachelor degrees within two years and four years.

Look at Legal and Typical Workloads

Does your campus have a legal range for maximum and minimum workload? What has the standard workload been in the past? How does your department workload compare with those of other departments on your campus and elsewhere? Consider increasing or decreasing instructor loads according to the needs of the department and the needs of the faculty.

Don't Automatically Replace Retiring Instructors

As much as we would like to honor our retiring colleagues, automatically replacing "dear old Joe" is not the way to do it. The goal of chairs must always be to improve the department. Too often we blindly hire a new faculty member to do exactly what "dear old Joe" did, even if what he was doing had long outlived its usefulness.

Enhance department productivity by determining your core and pruning your schedule. What are the courses that are "nice" but peripheral? Make sure that section productivity is maximized. Delete and combine sections. Reallocate weighted teaching units to positions where the department needs them the most. At this point, if you find that you do indeed need to replace Joe, do it with confidence.

Consider Team Teaching

Can some courses be team-taught by faculty both inside and outside your unit? Think about how much workload credit those team-teaching faculty should receive, whether it is credit for teaching the entire course or part credit.

Make Use of Teaching Assistants

Teaching assistants are especially valuable to busy professors and can be a real force multiplier. For faculty who insist they are already teaching the maximum number in their sections, offer them a teaching assistant to do mundane tasks such as responding to most e-mail questions, simple grading and tabulation, and entering student data for grading. This will free the faculty member to concentrate on more advanced student instructional needs. You can also assign advanced undergraduate and graduate students who are technology savvy to assist your faculty who may not yet be completely comfortable with the technology.

Make sure your teaching assistants are engaged in professional development to help them become better teachers. They should be receiving academic credit for the instruction they are receiving.

Chapter Ten

PROFESSIONAL DEVELOPMENT, PERSONNEL MANAGEMENT, AND HANDLING CHALLENGING PERSONNEL

Professor Galliard is faced, for the first time in her career, with the day-to-day challenges of professional development and personnel management that her dean has told her are part of her job as chair of the Linguistics Department. To her surprise, she has found that she enjoys helping her colleagues develop in the field, but she is finding the management of personalities somewhat difficult.

The linguistics faculty is quite collegial, except for one professor, Dr. Hagen, who seems to resist every suggestion for change. When she was his peer, she generally ignored his complaints and went about her teaching. But now she sees that any change to the curriculum, schedule, personnel procedures and expectations, or department manual and policies is loudly opposed by Dr. Hagen. He monopolizes department meetings with his complaints, and as a consequence, Professor Galliard is finding it difficult to accomplish even the smallest items on her agenda. The other faculty members are starting to grumble and are looking to her for leadership. She does not want to let this one bad apple spoil the barrel, as the saying goes, but she is at a loss as to what she can do.

Professor Galliard is not alone. This is representative of many personnel challenges faced by department chairs. One of the most common requests I hear during workshops for department chairs is "How can I handle challenging faculty?" All too often, just one or two difficult faculty can consume so much time and energy that the chair spends more time putting out fires than fueling the intellectual fires of talented faculty. Faculty talent and skills are precious resources that need to be developed and leveraged, as chairs have the fiduciary responsibility to manage all resources for the long-term benefit of the organization.

Your faculty are your department's greatest resource. The chair is responsible not only for managing problems but also for professional development and personnel management in general. The evaluation of faculty, their assignments, and their development as professionals are the key management function of department chairs. Decisions regarding hiring, tenure and promotion, and investments in faculty professional development will have long-term impacts on what students learn, developments in the service region, and institutional finances.

PROFESSIONAL DEVELOPMENT

The work of higher education typically takes place at the cutting edge of knowledge and technology. Professional development—the updating of skills and knowledge—is a fundamental necessity for fulfillment of the institutional mission. Chairs need to consider a panoply of factors with respect to the professional development of their faculty.

Teaching Competencies

Make a list of your full-time faculty and all of their teaching competencies. Most people have areas in which they are expert, as well as areas in which they can teach—especially in a pinch or as a sabbatical replacement. Bolster your teaching roster by professionally developing your faculty to teach in areas of anticipated need. For example, you might assign them to team-teach a course with an experienced faculty member or have them sit in on classes and review syllabi and assignments before they are assigned to teach the class.

Faculty Standouts

You can probably describe individuals you would consider the "best" faculty for a department and institution such as your own. But have you examined your reasons for these judgments? Ask yourself these questions: What characteristics do "best" faculty have? Why do you consider them superior? What would it take for your faculty to acquire the qualities exhibited by your "model" faculty if they are not already performing at that level? What qualities do you think they should exhibit in their teaching, scholarship, and service? In how they treat students, staff, and their colleagues? How high do you believe they should set the bar for themselves?

Peer Socialization

Position new hires around faculty you would like them to emulate. Peer socialization is a strong influence. New faculty are most affected by the people they happen to spend the most time around or individuals who seek out new faculty for the very purpose of influencing them. Think about where newcomers' offices are located, whom they will work with on projects, and whom they travel with to meetings and workshops—these are the people they will get to know best.

Positive Reinforcement

Public and private praise means something. So much of what we do is based on whatever enhances our self-esteem. A little attention and positive reinforcement from the chair can go a long way toward creating a positive work environment. Drop in on your faculty members during their office hours to tell them how much you appreciate the good work they have done. You will both get something out of the exchange.

Expectations

Link expectations for performance with the resources necessary to meet those expectations. For example, is it fair to ask junior faculty, who are typically paid the least, to assume cost obligations associated with their research and travel without a commitment from the administration to assist with those expenses?

Faculty Incentives

Create the incentives that will truly reward faculty for creating, growing, and strengthening valuable programs and projects. Is time what they want? If it's money, in what form? Do they want extra compensation? An extra summer teaching assignment? Do they prefer a research seed account that they can draw from to hire student workers or buy supplies or fund some travel? Or is recognition enough? If so, what kind of recognition is appropriate—an award, a public presentation, or kudos in a faculty meeting?

Faculty Opportunities

Help faculty identify where the best research, grant, or contract opportunities are. Young faculty, or more experienced faculty seeking to ramp up their scholarship, may not be in the network of funded faculty who feed each other this sort of information. They may not have the contacts in industry or with foundations or government grant officers who can give them a heads-up on what is coming down the road.

Support your faculty by funding them to attend national conferences where grant officers are reporting or where cutting-edge educators will be presenting. Ask your campus research officers to help your faculty make these contacts.

Every day, try to do something that will help at least one of your faculty grow professionally in his or her teaching, research, or service.

Funded Proposals

Keep a library of funded proposals. This will help your faculty draft their own proposals based on successful models. Be sure to include proposals from both on and off your campus.

National Meetings

Make sure that promising faculty are provided with the resources to attend meetings no less than one year in advance so that they can develop their presentations and submit them for consideration by program committees in a timely fashion. This allows them to write the best presentation possible and relieves the anxiety of "What if my proposal is accepted but I don't have the money to go?"

Professional Meetings

Bring teams of faculty to professional and scholarly meetings to learn about topics of departmentwide interest. Have them attend sessions together, debrief together, and report findings to the department. This supports the faculty and enriches your department.

Future Needs

The needs of education are always changing. In another decade, your department may need new faculty to teach in areas that are just now beginning to emerge. Explore now the skills they will need to serve your students, constituents, and society. Develop a plan for obtaining the resources to hire these people, or groom the staff you have in new directions.

Links with Practitioners

To link faculty with practitioners, consider employment of professionals from the field as "clinical faculty." There is a trend in higher education to employ practitioners in your department's field (either still working or retired) to mentor, connect, teach, advise, and liaison. These professionals have a wealth of contacts and practical experience that may benefit your faculty and students by providing the most hands-on professional development available in your region.

PERSONNEL MANAGEMENT

The evaluation of faculty and staff is an essential duty for department chairs. Done correctly, personnel management provides a framework for performance improvement. Done incorrectly, personnel management creates problems that interfere with the effectiveness of the organization.

Most chairs have had some involvement with faculty reviews as members of tenure and promotion review committees and of hiring and search committees. When they move into the main department office, however, chairs are typically expected to manage the entire personnel selection and review process as well as offer their independent evaluations of faculty and staff. Chairs need to think about the following issues when it comes to personnel management.

Unofficial Personnel "Pre-evaluations"

If your campus permits an "unofficial" review of files prepared for tenure and promotion, consider doing this. It will give applicants a heads-up one year earlier than the official tenure or promotion review and allow them time to plan.

Evaluation Norms

Construct a spreadsheet that you can use to gain a clearer picture of the normative ratings in your department. For each rating category, construct a quantitative scale so that you know what the mean and standard deviation are for ratings in the typical areas of teaching, scholarship, and service. Are your department mean and standard deviations typical across your institution? Are your faculty held to the same standards as faculty in other departments?

Model Personnel Files

Faculty who are about to prepare their dossiers for annual evaluation, tenure, or promotion review can benefit from consulting model personnel files. Place the files someplace where they can be monitored but where there is enough privacy that faculty members may view the dossier at leisure and make notes to improve their own files.

Performance Counseling

Don't just tell people what you think they did wrong. Help them improve by indicating what you think they can do better, and give them enough support so that they can accomplish the goals you lay out for them.

No Surprise Evaluations

Ensure that the results of performance reviews will not be a surprise to the faculty. Evaluation and counseling need to be ongoing—not once a year—based on the operationalization of department personnel policy.

Confidentiality

Find out your campus policy concerning maintaining your own written notes. In some states, any written record may be subpoenaed. In other states, notes maintained to jog memory are confidential. What is the law in your region?

Computer Records

Remember that everything that is e-mailed or otherwise crosses your office computer or institutionally provided laptop or mobile device can be recovered. Make sure you use institutionally provided electronic devices for official business only.

CHALLENGING PERSONNEL

Handling challenging personnel is an art. I am often asked, "What do I do to handle this kind of faculty member?" or "How can I manage personnel in my department so that I minimize problems?" If you have spent your life in teaching, management may be something you have never thought about—until now. If your faculty members are uniformly agreeable, consider yourself fortunate. Inevitably, however, you will sooner or later be involved in at least one challenge from a difficult colleague.

Here are two basic guidelines for behavior:

- Always take the high moral ground. Don't get into mud throwing; you will end up covered in mud yourself. And remember the old advertising slogan "Never let them see you sweat"? When dealing with personnel, it still rings true.

- Aim for a win-win outcome. If you win by wielding your authority and power, you will invariably lose some of your faculty in the process. If "win-win" is not possible, aim for a mutually acceptable solution. But recognize that sometimes only a mutually unacceptable outcome may be the best that you can achieve.

With these basics in mind, consider the following suggestions for effective personnel management. If you feel you need more, consult any of the many training courses and books on the subject.

Approaches to Use with Challenging Personnel

Faculty are under no legal obligation to be "nice." Often a simple "word to the wise" will resolve a situation. Some people, however, can just be plain difficult to deal with and can disrupt the smooth running of the department. For these people, you will likely have to exert some long-term effort.

For exceptionally challenging personnel, build a case. Get the evidence. Write it down. Establish a longitudinal history. The timeline and sequence of events is important. Get names and places along with details of what and when. Be forewarned: this can take years.

Begin by talking to them about their behavior—in the presence of a witness. If conversations or meetings are held in your office, have the door open enough to maintain confidentiality while ensuring security. Ask your office manager or assistant to keep an ear and eye open during such meetings.

If repeated counseling doesn't work, options may include waiting them out, isolating them, and transferring them. Faculty or staff who find it difficult to work in one environment may do just fine if they are moved to another environment, and challenging faculty do sooner or later move on. You may need to actively move "toxic" faculty to minimize departmental contagion.

Special cases include drug or alcohol abuse and discrimination that may be based on gender, sex, religion, race, or special needs. Consult with your dean and the Office of Human Resources because interventions may involve medical or governmental authorities.

Ethical and Legal Rights and Expectations

As the department's chief administrator, the chair is responsible for protecting the rights of the entire staff and faculty, including individuals who may not be among your favorite people. This also applies to the physical safety of those in your department. If you do not know what those rights are, educate yourself about them.

Administration, faculty, staff, and students are also expected to meet expectations for behavior and practice as set forth in institutional human resource documents, campus personnel handbooks, executive memorandums, and policies. College administrators, faculty, and staff are expected also to adhere to federal, state, and regional legal requirements that pertain to employment and the protection of legal rights.

Lack of Bias

There is more than one side to every personnel issue. Before you make a decision based on one person's complaint, ask all of the parties involved to tell you their side of the story. It is amazing what you can learn when you ask and listen—even when you're pretty sure you know everything that is going on in your department.

Legal and Historical Clarity

Personnel evaluations become part of permanent faculty records. They may be read by administrators, faculty outside of your department, and legal representatives. Write clearly enough for readers outside your department to understand—don't lapse into jargon that is incomprehensible to people outside your specialty. Provide sufficient supporting evidence and illustrations of abstract points so that the evaluations can be easily interpreted years or even decades later by people not currently at your institution and by those in the court system and federal and state government.

Critical Documents

Which of the many campus documents you will encounter do chairs really need to be familiar with? Chances are, the critical documents on your campus are institutional, college, and department personnel policy documents. State and federal law may also be relevant, depending on the personnel issue in question. Ask the best chairs on campus for the top three documents they think all chairs should know inside out.

Security of Files and Records

As chief administrator of your department, you are responsible for maintaining security. Keep a record of who has checked out personnel files and when. Track down any that are not returned promptly. Ensure that these files are protected from tampering and from pilferage of records, reports, letters, and memos.

Bullying and Harassment

Students, staff, faculty, and administration—no one has a right to bully or harass. Make sure you are familiar with the legal definitions of "harassment," "hostile work environment," and "unwelcome comments." If you are aware of possible harassment, you may be legally obligated to act. Inaction is sometimes illegal. Contact Human Resources and find out who is responsible for possible cases of harassment and bullying and how to report them.

CHAPTER ELEVEN

DEPARTMENTAL COMMUNICATION

Dr. Wong, hired thirty years ago as an assistant professor, has just been named chair of the Department of Electrical Engineering (EE) at Queens State College (QSC). The department has five tenure-track faculty (two assistant professors, two associate professors, and Dr. Wong herself, a full professor), five "instructional faculty" hired primarily to teach with no research expectations, and ten adjuncts hired to teach a course or two. These adjuncts are practicing engineers who mostly work full time in regional computer technology companies.

Dr. Wong has seen remarkable changes during her three decades of service. When she began her career at QSC, the labs were among the best in New York. Since then, however, the condition of the EE facilities have undermined what the faculty and students can do. They were fine for a curriculum designed primarily thirty years ago, but not for today's EE professionals. Most of her colleagues continue to concentrate on their specialized areas of scholarship, working as best they can with their students and pretty much keeping to themselves. She observes, "For most of us, our labs were our sanctuaries, and our students gave us meaning."

Chair Wong has observed dramatic facility and curricular changes in a number of science and engineering areas, but over the twenty years of the previous chair's administration, little changed for EE. She is determined to make things better for her faculty, her students, and the region. But how? She asks herself, "What did Chemical Engineering do? What did Mechanical Engineering do? Why did Biomedical Engineering get such a nice new building, labs, and equipment when the field didn't even exist when I started my career in EE?"

Dean Allen says that although he is supportive of EE, "I don't know what to give them. Every one of my departments in the College of Engineering wants better facilities, newer equipment, more faculty, and professional support. How do I know what they need—and the justification for allocation of resources to them—if they don't let me know through a most convincing case?"

He adds, "The sense I've had about EE over my ten years' tenure as their dean is that they are a 'good' department. They seem to graduate a reasonable number of majors. I don't hear of too many problems from them. But then again, I really don't know what they are doing that deserves accolades. They don't seem to stand out one way or the other. Frankly, I hear little about them from students, the community, my bosses, or the department itself."

With change a constant in the dynamic world of higher education, communication is key to understanding the necessity and reasoning behind department directions and administrative actions. Dr. Wong's and Dean Allen's experience with the Electrical Engineering Department is instructive in a number of ways.

From the dean's comments, it is clear that EE is not seen as a troubled department, nor is it perceived as a stellar department. It doesn't have enrollment problems, and the faculty buckle down to do their teaching jobs without causing waves for the dean. But as Dr. Wong has surmised, the lack of salience is a problem. Dr. Wong's predecessor may have seen the chair's job as primarily internal—that is, to take care of EE's students in the best possible way, given the lab situation. Yet as the dean's comments illustrate, in the absence of effective communication that EE was not realizing the potential contributions it could make to students with better labs and newer equipment, the dean's priorities were elsewhere.

Chair Wong sees that her colleagues in other engineering departments have gotten nice new buildings, labs, and equipment. Now, perhaps, she will ramp up the communications necessary for EE to see a revitalized future. She begins to plan a consistent and persistent communication campaign. Dr. Wong hopes that by giving Dean Allen a clear picture of how essential EE is not only to the College of Engineering but also to the university and its service region, and by allowing friends and supporters of EE to help the department make its case to decision leaders and influential friends of the university, her efforts will lead to a much better program for her students.

EFFECTIVE COMMUNICATION

Effective communication is important for many reasons. Shared governance requires trust. It also requires solid information on which to make decisions or to defer responsibility for decision making to others. Good communication gives faculty and administration confidence in the work that they are doing together.

The basic rule of good communication—whether you are speaking to a student, a colleague, your dean, or a community partner—is to be an active listener. Listen carefully and echo your understanding so that the people you speak with know that you care enough about them to pay attention to what they say.

Build trust through respectful communication. Maintain confidentiality at all times. Chairs have access to all sorts of sensitive personal information. Protect that information, just as you would want others to protect information about yourself. Never gossip or convey a sense that you are willing to listen to gossip. There is no place for rumor in the academy.

Choose your message carefully. There is no need to communicate to your department about every issue that passes across your desk. In fact, your faculty and students are counting on you to protect them from the "administrivia" that they likely see as a large part of the chair's job.

Finally, be aware that communication is largely nonverbal. Always remember that even without doing anything, you are sending a message, because as chair, you are the public face of your department. Always carry yourself with the demeanor that you would like the public to equate with your department and its students and faculty. Model the characteristics that best represent the department.

Connect Through Communication

As chair, you have the opportunity to connect with your colleagues inside the department and with your dean, students, and community constituents. Friendmaking is part of your job. There is a reason that officials are often provided with an account to use for "social purposes." It is a truism that friendmaking typically precedes fundraising.

Communicating wisely helps everyone understand your department's agenda, issues, and accomplishments. The choice of issues that you prioritize as worthy of your time and focus communicates information about your agenda and your competency.

Build a Communication Plan for Your Department

A good communication plan must provide useful information to important constituents such as your dean, your faculty, other departments, and the community. Be sure to include faculty and student accomplishments, as well as future plans. Send this information to the department, the college, the university, the community, and other interested constituents.

If you decide to issue a periodical department newsletter, make sure it is regular enough—monthly or quarterly, perhaps—to develop a momentum. People will look forward to reading about your accomplishments. Keep your department in the minds of decision makers with positive news at least several times per term.

Use Social Media

Do you tweet on Twitter? Are you on Facebook? Social media are ubiquitous among the young and very popular with almost everyone else these days. You are probably already using mass e-mails to get information out to your students, but you may not be taking full advantage of the power of social media to communicate—not only with students but also with community groups. Consider appointing a student worker or graduate student to handle social media relations for the department.

Communicate Through Department Meetings

Department meetings are your most important opportunity to communicate your plans to faculty and staff, who will be judging your performance largely by what you say and how you say it. Select your agenda items wisely—remember that not every problem is a problem, and some are actually opportunities for discussion.

Use everyone's time efficiently. Demonstrate knowledge of *Robert's Rules of Order* if necessary. Listen respectfully. Check to make sure everyone understands what has been discussed. When you come to a decision, do what you say you will do.

Actively Seek New Connections

Always be looking for ways to help not just your faculty but also your constituents inside and outside of your institution. Meet with key constituents in your service region. Let them know you care. Keep an eye open for funding, scholarship, and service opportunities. Make the connections that will benefit your faculty and students. Introduce faculty with appropriate skills to constituents who need their talents.

Connect with Important People in Your Task Environment

Draw up a list of services that faculty and students perform for your constituents, and keep track of the number of hours that they devote to the community and the names of their supervisors. Build a list of friends of the department.

The more people who know all the wonderful things your department is doing, the better. Conduct an environmental scan of your organization and its constituents to find out who are the most important people or groups in your task environment, including key officers on campus. Make appointments to get to know them and discuss what you can do for each other. Invite them to faculty meetings to provide an overview of what they and their key staff do. Faculty will also have an opportunity to communicate. This helps everyone feel informed and connected.

Connect with Your Dean

What does your dean want you to accomplish? Ask your dean for a list of goals he or she would like your department to achieve each year, and share your own goals. Make sure that all goals are prioritized, operationalized, and discussed by your department with your dean in attendance.

Connect Faculty with Faculty

Encourage faculty to work with colleagues. At each department meeting, ask one or two faculty members to tell colleagues what they are doing in classes, scholarship, or service. This kind of sharing can stimulate many new ideas and enliven your department.

REACHING OUT

New chairs typically feel overwhelmed with new responsibilities and tasks. There is a real tendency to hunker down for the duration and feel that you have to get it all sorted out and done on your own. In fact, the solution—and a major component of effective departmental communication—is in sharing the load. Reach out to others and find out how you can help each other.

Reach Out to Other Chairs

Leadership is easy when the variables are well known and clearly understood. When the formula for action is well accepted, leadership is a cinch. Departmental and institutional leadership can be difficult is because administrators often work on the edges of what is well known, and direction is not firmly set.

The solution is to triangulate information with others in your position. Actively build communication with the best chairs on campus. They have already sorted out many of the issues you are facing. In almost every case, they will be your best sources of information and guidance. Be sure to talk to several individuals—opinions always vary about what is best.

If the chairs on your campus do not get together regularly, formally or informally, explore this possibility. Find out whether or not this effort would be supported by your dean and provost.

Reach Out to Faculty

It's also a good idea to legitimize your cohorts. Make appointments to visit faculty in their offices. Ask them to tell you about their issues, and ask what you can do to help them.

Meet with small groups of your faculty outside of large department meetings. Large meetings are often dominated by the highest-profile or most insistent faculty and issues, and junior faculty may feel vulnerable. Hold separate meetings with all part-time faculty and with assistant professors, associate professors, and full professors. Find out what is on their personal agendas and how they feel you might be of help.

Reach Out to Students

Work with the admissions office to reach out to potential students and also to make friends with students and the community so that they learn about what your department does. Connecting with the community is an essential part of the chair's boundary-spanning responsibilities.

You can also ask your admissions office for the names of your primary feeder schools. What high schools and community colleges provide most of your majors? Find out the names of key personnel who direct students into higher education, and connect with them. Invite them to campus and make it clear to them how much they mean to you.

Visit your student majors club regularly. Bring student leaders to national and regional conferences. Make professional socialization a priority. Assign a major club adviser who cares about students and who will spend significant time with them.

Meet with graduating majors at least once a year. Ask them which classes were their best or their favorites and which could stand improvement. Do this before you sign off on their graduation check sheets, and they will be sure to come in for the appointment.

Keep a list of internship opportunities with specific contact information that students can refer to. If you feel it might be useful and cost-efficient to place a faculty member in charge of internships, make sure that that person checks in with internship site coordinators to see how your students are doing and if there is anything else you can do for them. Not only is the internship an entrée for your students, but it is also your department's contact with that organization.

CHAPTER TWELVE

STUDENT DEVELOPMENT

The college catalogue states, "The Department of Health Care Management puts students first." The new chair, Dr. Dobrov, was proud of that fact: his department had continually given close attention to its majors. But now he suddenly realized that this student-centered reputation might actually have contributed to the department's problems. This year, it had an abundance of new majors and not enough faculty to serve them.

With so many new majors, with health care so salient in the national dialogue, and with limited budgets in recent years constraining the addition of faculty and support staff, Dr. Dobrov realized that changes were needed—and fast. Two senior faculty would be retiring this year, leaving one assistant, three associate professors, one full professor, and the chair. "One of our senior faculty who is retiring was our primary adviser," explained Dr. Dobrov. "She liked working with the students even though she wasn't really up to date with the latest advances in the field. I'll get to hire one new faculty member next year, but chances are it will have to be in a health care management area associated with economics or information technology."

Dr. Dobrov had a lot on his mind. "We've got an additional 20 percent undergraduate enrollment and 30 percent more graduate majors from just two years ago. But with our recent retirements, and with no money to hire new faculty and staff, we're stretched so thin that I am afraid we're not communicating with our students the way we should." He sighed.

"With so many changes due to health care reform and technology," he concluded, "we have had to completely revamp our curriculum; our prerequisites in particular have changed due to new technology-rich course content required for our seniors. I am afraid, however, that we are creating problems for ourselves and for our students who don't know how much things have changed."

Indeed, there have been so many changes in the health care management major in recent years, says Dr. Dobrov, that even the campus career center is out of touch. The new chair wonders how the department can maintain its student-centered reputation when there are so many new jobs in health care management but the career center knows so little about how to connect graduates with employers.

The case of the Department of Health Care Management illustrates an all-too-common problem for academic units with growing enrollments unmatched by student support resources. Just about every school and its units say, "We put students first." But how well do departments communicate with students? Does the department leave communication up to each faculty and staff member, or is the chair involved to ensure that effective and timely communication takes place? Does the department communicate with students in the way they are accustomed, or are we depending on outdated methods of getting our message across?

Dr. Dobrov is facing issues common to many department leaders today. How do we reach out to students most effectively with limited resources? How do we help them learn what they need to know to graduate and connect with future employers? What's the best way to advise them and also get the information we need from them so that we can change to meet their needs?

A PROACTIVE APPROACH

Some departments give up, leaving communication with students largely to individual faculty and staff initiative. Other departments take a proactive approach to student communication by planning to maximize advising services and reach out to students to give them the information they need as well as to gain feedback from them that is helpful in planning for the future. Chairs interested in enhancing department effectiveness working with their students should consider the following points.

Review Elective and Entry-Level Courses

Electives are the primary means through which your department communicates with potential majors about what your department is all about. Are your elective and entry-level courses attractive to potential majors? Are these courses taught by faculty who communicate well with students, who will then be attracted to your department? The number of your majors is a resource, since it is virtually guaranteed enrollments and provides a source of student workers and graduate students.

Meet with Students

Have a mandatory exit meeting with seniors before you sign off on their graduation check sheet. Even a five- or ten-minute meeting with your seniors just before they graduate allows you to gather crucial information for the future. For example, what do they feel were their best classes? What are their immediate plans after graduation? Be sure to collect their contact information so you can maintain your connection as they enter professional life.

Develop Student Leaders

Consider appointing your best students to appropriate committees. The effect student representatives can have on the process of department-level committee work is truly amazing. Such appointments also enable students to see how shared governance operates and to see faculty in a different light.

Sponsor Student Attendance at Professional Association Meetings

Engage students in professional association groups specifically designed for young professionals. Have students present a report to the department as part of their trip responsibilities. If finances are too tight to support attendance at national meetings, realize that travel to regional meetings usually requires less expense.

Stimulate Student Engagement with the Community

Your students' positive interactions with the community will work in both directions: they provide good public relations for your department and good professional contact for students. Offer credit or extra credit for student service to organizations relevant to the student's major interest area.

You may also consider appointing members of your student majors club to staff an annual development drive. Potential donors and alumni often prefer connecting with energetic, engaging students. Again, not only does this help students make connections, but it may also help your department's bottom line.

Make the Majors Club Worthwhile

Your students' majors club is the means through which they are socialized into your profession. Arrange meetings for your majors with successful alumni, organize trips to professional conferences, and introduce your best students to professional contacts you have in your field. Coordinate service work relevant to your profession. Assign students important work, such as hosting alumni and potential majors at social events. Your best majors may be good ambassadors for phonathons or other fundraising events.

Appoint a faculty liaison to the majors club who cares and wants to be there. Your majors club should have a faculty liaison who communicates well and is motivated to help students.

Connect with Student Affairs

Too often faculty and academic administrators work solely inside their own bubble. Yet if we are truly concerned with our students, we should coordinate our work with colleagues charged with student education outside of our classrooms. Get to know your student affairs administrators and their key staff. Ask what you can do to help them with their work. Are there a small number of staff who work with your students?

Connect with Alumni

Grow your relationships with alumni so that they can connect with your graduates and help them grow professionally and personally. Being mentored by professional role models is an ideal way of communicating to graduates the value of what they are learning in your department.

ADVISING

Advising is a key area in which to connect with students. They are coming to you for answers—this is a great opportunity to put your department in the best light possible by taking them seriously and making sure you serve them well.

Ninety percent of student questions are routine and can be handled by trusted majors and graduate students through office hours appointments, online questions and answers, and phone calls. For the remaining 10 percent, you will need someone to advise who not only knows the policies but can also communicate well with students.

Use Peer Advisers

Consider appointing graduate students as peer advisers. This frees faculty from the most routine advising duties and also helps young professionals mentor their more junior peers. They can refer more difficult questions to faculty. Make sure your advisers maintain records of all student-adviser proceedings.

Schedule Regular Advising Sessions

If advising is required by your institution or department, set up regular advising sessions. Large or small group sessions for majors can minimize the "I didn't know I needed to take that" problems just before graduation time and can make students feel they have been well taken care of by the department.

Create Good Graduation Requirement Check Sheets

An easily understood list of required and elective courses and prerequisites is a great way to communicate to students what is most important for them to know in your majors. Who in your institution has the clearest, most concise summary of major requirements? Base your own department check sheets on these best examples.

CHAPTER THIRTEEN

STRATEGIC POSITIONING

Dr. Nomura, the new chair of the Department of Education at one of California's large state universities, is worried. The department had been an important part of the university since its origins as a normal school. As the state grew, many normal schools became state colleges and then universities. Demand for teachers was steady, and education departments thrived, with consistent enrollments that fed the state's demand for teachers and school administrators. But with Proposition 13 (a severe cap on property taxes implemented in 1978), hard economic times, and diminishing population increases in the Golden State, the demand for teachers and school administrators dried up seemingly overnight.

With further budget reductions in the immediate and foreseeable future, Dr. Nomura must come up with a plan. He sees that other departments are apparently weathering the state budget storm rather well. Kinesiology, for instance, has maintained its enrollments by offering new curriculum to prepare more of its majors for both physical therapy and physical therapy assistant jobs in high demand for the region's aging population. Philosophy seems to be doing all right as well. Dr. Nomura wonders if it has something to do with how well that department is placed in both the campus budget advisory committee and the academic senate, where the chair is a well-respected Philosophy faculty member.

Then there is Agriculture, which had been under the gun in previous California recessions. Now, with its abundance of external grants that play off of the department's strengths in bioagricultural engineering, so many of its faculty can access external funds that they seem be much less reliant on state legislative appropriations to pay their bills. Dr. Nomura plans to speak to chairs of Kinesiology, Philosophy, and Agriculture to learn how he can position Education for the future.

The department chair is authorized to get people together. This includes not only the faculty, staff, and students in your department but also faculty and staff throughout the institution and your service constituents. The authority of your office allows you to position the department so that it can be among the first in line to learn about and acquire resources, information, and opportunities for your faculty and students. A well-positioned department is at the top of the barrel, not at the bottom—and in a perfect place to hear about campus discussion in the draft stage, before it becomes policy.

POSITIONING YOUR DEPARTMENT POLITICALLY

Much of the chair's work is getting talented members of the department in the right places at the right time. Like a coach who puts the skilled player in the space where the action is or soon will be taking place, the chair needs to position faculty and students where they can benefit the most. When decisions are being made, when resources are allocated, when information is made public, it is always better for your department to be a significant part of the process than to be advised after the fact about decisions that have already been made by others.

Knowing where organizations are considering investing their resources, when requests for proposals will be made public, and what decision makers really want as opposed to what they are able to express publicly gives your department faculty and students opportunities that others who are less intimately involved in decision making do not have.

The realities of real-world funding mean that proactive chairs must work hard to position their departments for future success. Departments that are positioned well politically can influence decisions, have the information they need to navigate turbulent patches, and succeed in times when other departments falter. It is during dark times that the relatively few bright lights appear to shine the brightest.

By heeding the following advice, chairs will position their units and faculty so that they will have greater impact on their department's future.

Understand the Assessment Metrics

Know what metrics are being used to assess the value of departments: enrollments, external funding, curriculum, expertise, or programs that are needed for the service region, employers, or legislators. If "centrality to the mission of the institution" is the key criterion for the determination of high-priority departments, how is "centrality" defined? Once you have determined these criteria, do what you can to meet them.

Know What a Strong Department Looks Like

What departments on campus are the strongest? Positioning your department implies that you know where it is and where it should be. If you have an idea what the best departments look like, you'll have an idea where to position your own unit.

The strongest departments generally have curriculum that is in demand, as manifested in consistent high enrollments. Strong departments have greater financial autonomy because they have annual funds, extrainstitutional grants and contracts, recognized expertise required for students and other constituents, and a strong reputation as good citizens in the institution's shared governance. This reputation is reflected in the department's representation on the institution's most influential governance committees.

Be Prepared

Well-positioned departments are always prepared for what is just over the horizon. Find out what data will be needed so that you may accumulate in advance information you and others acting for the department require for decision making. Draft documents well in advance of deadlines for turning in finished reports. Stock the resources you will need for future investments. Prepare personnel so that they have the knowledge and skills they will need before they must act on behalf of the department.

Conduct an Environmental Scan

It pays to understand your environment and what you will be dealing with. Examine other departments, divisions of the institution, the community, institutional and community leaders, and state and national directions. Outside of your department, where are the greatest potential benefits and rewards? Where are the greatest threats or risks? They could be national associations, accrediting bodies, alumni groups, businesses, or networks of experts from other institutions. Get your faculty connected with each of them, preferably in some leadership capacity.

Know Where to Find the Data You Need

Strong departments know where to find the data they need to bolster their case. Departments must justify why they deserve support. Chairs who know where the data are and access those data to make their case on behalf of the department can position the unit far better than chairs who are unwilling or unable to make data-based arguments on behalf of their departments.

Make Your Department Flexible and Helpful

Strong departments are nimble and flexible. They have curriculum ready to go when needed. They have course and section scheduling flexibility. Chairs know where additional student enrollments can be added, at what time and days. Their faculty can teach in a second and third area of instruction if needed. They have graduate students, part-time adjuncts, emeritus faculty, and clinical professionals available to help out if needed.

STAYING CLOSE TO DECISION MAKING AND DECISION MAKERS

Do what you can to put yourself and your faculty close enough to where decisions will be made and where resources may be available that your department can be a part of the action. Chairs who understand the groups on and off campus who are important to the department, its faculty, its students, and its future can use their position as official liaisons help their faculty and students be part of groups that make decisions. By helping your department members get to know officials in agencies, foundations, and community and business groups, you will also facilitate resource flow into your unit. This is how to position yourself and your faculty close to those who can make a difference.

Position Your Faculty

Get your best faculty on important committees. What are the most important committees in your college or university? Get your trusted faculty on those committees, preferably in leadership positions.

Position Yourself

Get known by important people in important organizations. Chairs need to serve as liaisons between constituents (who have needs and resources) and their faculty (who have talent and need resources). Find out who those constituents are in the community, on the national scene, and in your own institution, and explore how you might be able to help each other.

Understand the Decision Process

Visualize a flowchart for each important decision to be made in your institution. Who are the key officers in decisions? From whom do they get their information? What are the key committees on campus? How can you help position key faculty to be on those committees, especially in a leadership capacity?

Create an Advisory Board

You can use emeritus faculty, alumni, and friends of the department to help you gain access so that you can position yourself and your faculty. Create an advisory board composed of campus, community, and alumni leaders and friends. Where appropriate, include graduates who are professionally successful and employers of your graduates. Potential advisory board members will often be flattered that they have been asked to serve and pleased to have some official connection with your institution.

CHAPTER FOURTEEN

UNDERSTANDING YOUR INSTITUTION AND YOUR ROLE AS DEPARTMENT CHAIR

Now that you have some idea of what is involved in the work of a department chair, you can take some time to understand your unit and its place within the institution and the environment in which it operates. This questionnaire is designed to get you started on that process and to prepare you with the background and information needed to manage and lead your department. Write out your responses on separate sheets of paper, taking as much time as you need to answer each question. Keep your answers handy, and refer to them or revise them as necessary. They will serve you well throughout your term as chair.

1. My Institution

1.1. In the Carnegie classification system, my institution is classified as what kind of institution (doctorate-granting university, baccalaureate college, and so on)?

1.2. Is my institution public or private? For-profit or not-for-profit?

1.3. When was it established?

1.4. My institution faces many of the same internal and external challenges and opportunities that other institutions face in this day and age. List its primary *external* challenges.

1.5. List its primary *internal* challenges.

1.6. List its primary *opportunities.*

2. My Role as Chair

2.1. Make a list of the previous chairs and their length of service.

2.2. Do my department faculty expect me to lead and manage aggressively for productivity? Rate this on a scale of 1 to 5 (1 = faculty do not expect aggressive chair leadership and management, 5 = faculty do expect aggressive leadership and management). Why have I given this rating?

2.3. How strongly will my faculty support my vigorous efforts to improve department productivity? Rate this on a scale of 1 to 5 (1 = weak faculty support for productivity growth; 5 = strong faculty support for productivity growth). Why have I given this rating?

2.4. Does my dean expect me to lead and manage aggressively for productivity? Rate this on a scale of 1 to 5 (1 = dean does not expect aggressive chair leadership and management; 5 = dean does expect aggressive chair leadership and management). Why have I given this rating?

2.5. Are my dean's expectations for my performance as chair clear? Rate this on a scale of 1 to 5 (1 = job expectations are unclear; 5 = job expectations are clear).

2.6. Will I receive a formal evaluation of my performance as chair from my dean? If so, what criteria will be used for this evaluation?

2.7. What is the likelihood that my annual compensation will be affected by my performance as chair? Rate this on a scale of 1 to 5 (1 = unlikely; 5 = likely).

2.8. Identify the five most important people or offices in my campus environment that have an effect on my department's performance. Do I interact regularly with each of them? Describe the interactions with each.

2.9. Identify the five most important people, offices, or organizations that have an effect on my department's performance. Do I interact regularly with each of them? Describe the interactions with each.

2.10. Name two departments like mine that I consider exemplary. What three components of each of these departments do I admire most?

2.11. What are my top three goals as chair this year? I will know that I have achieved these goals by looking at what particular indicators for each goal?

3. Governance

3.1. Draw the organizational flowchart for my institution.

3.2. Indicate the key administrative officers at my institution, their backgrounds, and their years of service.

3.3. Describe the agenda for the president.

3.4. Describe the agenda for the provost.

3.5. Describe the dean's agenda.

3.6. Faculty influence in my institution is primarily exercised through which committees and organizations?

3.7. Identify the key department committees. Then describe how membership on each committee is determined. Which faculty have voting rights? Are committee votes public or confidential?

3.8. Is there a faculty union that is the sole bargaining agent for faculty contracts? Is the union an open or closed shop? Are dues automatically or voluntarily paid from faculty paychecks?

3.9. Name the vice presidents' and vice chancellor's divisions. Do they meet with the head of my institution as a group? If so, what is it called (e.g., cabinet, board)? How often does it meet?

3.10. To whom do chairs in my institution report? How often do they meet as a group with their administrative head?

3.11. Do all chairs on campus meet? If so, how often do they meet? Who chairs this meeting?

3.12. At the department level, is the chair elected or appointed? Is the chair officially considered a member of the administration? Terms or appointments are for how many months?

3.13. Compared to their faculty, are chairs paid more, paid the same, or given a stipend or other additional compensation? If chairs receive additional compensation, how is the amount of that compensation determined?

4. Budget and Expenses

4.1. Who is my dean's budget officer?

4.2. In my institution, what is the most important factor that determines how much money is available for distribution into unit budgets (enrollments, state allocations, allocation formulas, tuition and fees, contracts and grants, donations, other)?

4.3. If a funding formula largely determines allocations to units, what is the funding formula?

4.4. Describe the budget allocation process for my institution.

4.5. Describe the annual budgeting process calendar. What offices does it involve?

4.6. What has my institution's total operating budget been for the last three to five years?

4.7. What is my department's percentage of that total operating budget (including personnel costs) for each of those years?

4.8. What are the primary reasons for fluctuations in that proportion of the total of my institution's budget allocated to my department?

4.9. Give a breakdown of the total operating budget, indicating the dollar amounts of endowments, grants, and contracts. How much are tuition and fees? By what percentage have they changed over the past five years?

4.10. Does my institution receive state support? If so, how much does that amount to annually? On what formula or factors is that based?

4.11. For the last three to five years, what percentage of my department's operating budget has gone to pay for personnel, with the remainder offsetting nonpersonnel expenses?

4.12. On the income side of the budget, what percentage has come from state allocations, from tuition and fees, and from grants and contracts?

4.13. Does my institution's policy permit carryforwards of unspent funds?

4.14. What has my department's budget been over the past five years? Who allocates funds for personnel, operations, travel and professional development, and student assistants? What process is used for these allocations? On what criteria and factors are they based?

4.15. Are departments incentivized to save and make their own money? If so, through what incentives?

4.16. Who within the department allocates funds to faculty and programs? What process is used for these allocations?

4.17. Each of the department's programs receive what percentage of operational funding (including personnel dollars)? Over the past three to five years, how have these percentages varied? What are the highest-priority department programs? Over the past three to five fiscal years, have funds been shifted to high-priority programs?

5. Faculty Development, Workload, and Schedule

5.1. Who are my most important faculty this year? How will I support the professional development of each of them this year?

5.2. The normal workload for faculty is how many classes?

5.3. What is the legal or campus policy regarding the minimum and maximum number of classes that must be taught by full-time faculty each year?

5.4. How are classes offered: primarily face to face, online, or a combination of both? What percentage of online classes is synchronous? During the past five years, has the percentage of online and blended class sections grown? If so, by what percentages of sections?

5.5. Over the past five years, has the percentage of sections taught by full-time faculty increased or decreased? By what percentages of sections? Is the remainder taught by part-time faculty?

5.6. How is the department instructional schedule constructed? Who is responsible for constructing the teaching schedule?

5.7. Is the chair responsible for developing performance expectations for faculty relative to scholarship and service? If not, who is?

5.8. How are teaching expectations typically described? How are they measured or operationalized?

5.9. How are scholarship expectations typically described? How are they measured or operationalized?

5.10. How are service expectations typically described? How are they measured or operationalized?

5.11. What are the highest curriculum priorities in my department?

5.12. How often is the department curriculum reviewed for relevance and need for change?

5.13. How often is the instructional schedule reviewed for relevance and need for change?

Resources

Web Sites

American Council on Education Department Chair Online Resource Center, http://www.acenet.edu/resources/chairs/
Jossey-Bass Department Chair Leadership Institute, http://www.depart mentchairs.org/

Newsletters

The Department Chair: A Resource for Academic Administrators
The Jossey-Bass Department Chair Insider
The Department Chair: A Resource for Academic Administrators

Books

Barr, Margaret J. *Academic Administrator's Guide to Budgets and Financial Management*. San Francisco: Jossey-Bass, 2002.
Bess, James L., and Jay R. Dee. *Understanding College and University Administration: Theories for Effective Policy and Practice* (2 vol.). Sterling, Va.: Stylus, 2008.
Buller, Jeffrey. *The Essential Department Chair: A Practical Guide to College Administration*. Bolton, Mass.: Anker, 2006.
Chu, Don, and Sally Veregge. *The California State University Department Chair Survey Report*. Spring 2002. http://www.calstate.edu/AcadSen/Records/Reports/CSU_Chairs_survey_report.pdf
Covey, Stephen. *The 7 Habits of Highly Effective People: Powerful Lessons in Personal Change* (rev. ed.). New York: Simon & Schuster, 2004.
Creswell, John W., and others. *The Academic Chairperson's Handbook*. Lincoln: University of Nebraska Press, 1990.
Diamond, Robert M. (Ed.). *Field Guide to Academic Leadership*. San Francisco: Jossey-Bass, 2002.
Gmelch, Walter H. *Leadership Self-Assessment*. Bolton, Mass.: Anker, 1993.

Gmelch, Walter H. *Understanding the Challenges of Department Chairs.* Bolton, Mass.: Anker. 1993.

Gmelch, Walter H., and Val Miskin. *Chairing an Academic Department* (2nd ed.). Madison, Wis.: Atwood, 2002.

Hecht, I.W.D., and others. *The Department Chair as Academic Leader.* Washington, D.C.: American Council on Education/Oryx Press, 1999.

Higgerson, Mary Lou, and Teddi A. Joyce. *Effective Leadership Communication: A Guide for Department Chairs and Deans for Managing Difficult Situations and People.* Bolton, Mass.: Anker, 2007.

Leaming, Deryl R. *Academic Leadership: A Practical Guide to Chairing the Department* (2nd ed.). San Francisco: Jossey-Bass, 2007.

Lucas, Ann F. *Leading Academic Change: Essential Roles for Department Chairs.* San Francisco: Jossey-Bass, 2000.

Seldin, Peter, and Mary Lou Higgerson. *The Administrative Portfolio: A Practical Guide to Improved Administrative Performance and Personnel Decisions.* Bolton, Mass.: Anker, 2002.

Sorcinelli, Mary Deane, and others. *Creating the Future of Faculty Development.* Bolton, Mass.: Anker, 2006.

Tucker, Allan. *Chairing the Academic Department: Leadership Among Peers* (3rd ed.). New York: American Council on Education/Macmillan, 1992.

Wheeler, Daniel W., Jack H. Schuster, and Associates. *Enhancing Faculty Careers: Strategies for Development and Renewal.* San Francisco: Jossey-Bass, 1990.

Wheeler, Daniel W., and others. *The Academic Chairperson's Handbook* (2nd ed.). San Francisco: Jossey-Bass, 2008.

REFERENCES

Chu, Don, and Sally Veregge. *The California State University Department Chair Survey Report*. Spring 2002. http://www.calstate.edu/AcadSen/Records/Reports/CSU_Chairs_survey_report.pdf

Covey, Stephen. *The 7 Habits of Highly Effective People: Powerful Lessons in Personal Change* (rev. ed.). New York: Simon & Schuster, 2004.

Gmelch, Walter H. "Department Chair Development." Workshop presented at the American Council on Education Department Chair Workshops, San Diego, Calif., 2000.

Meyer, John W., and Brian Rowan. "Formal Structure as Myth and Ceremony." *American Journal of Sociology*, 1977, *83*, 340–363.

Perlmutter, Daniel. "Spotting Your Enemies." *Chronicle of Higher Education*, Nov. 7, 2010. http://chronicle.com/article/Spotting-Your-Faculty-Enemies/125289/

The Author

Don Chu is coauthor of the *California State University Department Chair Survey Report* and dean of the College of Education, Health, and Human Services at California State University, San Marcos. Prior to his current position, he was dean of the College of Professional Studies at the University of West Florida, served nine years as chair of the Department of Kinesiology at the University of California, Chico, and was a California State University Executive Fellow in 1999–2000. Don may be contacted at dchu@csusm.edu.

INDEX

Page references followed by *fig* indicate an illustrated figure.

Jossey-Bass Department Chair Leadership Institute Online Seminar Series

www.departmentchairs.org

The Jossey-Bass Department Chair Leadership Institute is proud to offer practical, completely interactive 90-minute online sessions for department chairs. These seminars are designed to provide the professional enrichment, networking opportunities, and essential training that most department chairs never have the chance to experience but desperately need. The benefits include

- You can attend from anywhere! Taking place completely over the Web, the seminar series is wherever you are. All sessions begin at 11:30 EST, and all you need to participate is a computer with internet access.
- Enjoy access to recorded sessions for six months after the event. Can't attend on the live date? No problem-you can review the content whenever it's most convenient for *you.*
- Interact with and learn directly from dynamic speakers and peers.
- Receive complimentary resources plus special discounts on Jossey-Bass and Wiley books and periodicals-good for professional development titles *and* discipline-specific resources.
- Cost-effective pricing, early bird discounts, and zero travel make this one of the most economical professional development opportunities available to department chairs.
- Live interaction and networking with other department chairs and professionals just like yourself!

For more information and to register, simply visit **www.department chairs.org**. While you're there, be sure to sign up for our free bi-monthly e-newsletter, *The Jossey-Bass Department Chair Insider.*